2222 Interesting, Wacky & Crazy Facts

The Knowledge Encyclopedia To Win Trivia

Scott Matthews

1. A multi-millionaire named Forrest Fenn has hidden a treasure valued between one to three million dollars in the Rocky Mountains, and to find it, you must solve his riddle. So far, no one has done it or found the treasure.

2. The director of the 1980 horror film 'Cannibal Holocaust' had to prove in court that the actors were still alive and didn't get killed during the movie.

3. At the age of 15, Anne Mackosinski managed to invent a flashlight that is powered solely by the hand's body heat. She later created a headlamp that's also powered by body heat.

4. Ninjas didn't wear black. According to the ninja museums in Japan, the best color to wear during the night time for ninjas was actually dark navy blue.

5. Red pandas use their long bushy tails to balance whenever they're in the trees. Their tails were also used to cover themselves for warmth in the winter.

6. During job interviews, Google doesn't ask for GPA or test scores from their candidates, because they don't correlate at all with success at the company.

7. Only 5% of Norway's financial transactions are done in cash. In fact, it's possible that by 2020 Norway could be completely cash-free.

8. In the movie the Matrix, Neo's passport expires on September 11th, 2001.

9. The Ben Franklin effect is a psychological phenomenon where someone who has done a favor for someone else is more likely to do another favor for that person than they would be if they had received a favor from that person.

10. You can actually reshape some babies' ears. Some of them have a condition called lidling, where the top part of the cartilage in the ear is basically folded over so the top ridge is kind of rounded over. However there's a mold, called EarWell, that can change the shape of your baby's ear in approximately six weeks.

11. There are more bicycles than people in Copenhagen, and five times as many bicycles as cars. Over 50% of city dwellers

commute by bicycle, and over 41% arrive at their place of work or study by bike.

12. In the United States, the government can legally read any emails that you have that are over 180 days old without a warrant. The Electronic Communications Privacy Act was enacted long before everybody had email and the law still allows them to do this.

13. India-based Graviky Labs has found a way to use pigment from carbon soot-polluted air to make pens, oil-based paints, and spray paint. A single Air Ink pen contains 30 to 40 minutes of carbon emissions from a single car.

14. As of 2019, Apple has sold over one billion iPhones.

15. NASA's robotic spacecraft, Juno, traveled a total distance of 1.74 billion miles (2.9 billion km) to arrive on the planet Jupiter. It launched from Cape Canaveral on August 5th, 2011, and arrived on Jupiter on July 4th, 2016.

16. In California, on July 30th, 2016, 42-year-old paratrooper Luke Aikens became the first person to jump from an airplane without a parachute or wingsuit. He jumped 25,000 feet (7,620 meters) to Earth, setting a world record for the highest jump. He landed safely in a 100-square-foot (9 square meter) net. That's about one third the size of a football field.

17. According to a study done in 2008, smells can influence our dreams. Subjects of the study where the scent of roses were infused when they were dreaming gave nearly all of them pleasant dreams. However, when the air around those subjects was infused with the smell of rotten eggs while they were dreaming, they had negative dreams.

18. There's an inn in Idaho called the Dog Bark Park Inn, where guests can stay in the world's largest beagle. You enter the body of the beagle from a second-story deck. Up another level into the head of the dog is a loft, and there's an additional sleeping space and a cozy alcove in the muzzle.

19. In 1958, Robert Lane from New York City named his son Winner, and later another son, Loser. Winner ended up as a criminal with a lengthy arrest record, and his son loser went on to prep school

on a scholarship, graduated from college, and joined the New York Police Department.

20. The crew of Apollo 15 placed a small aluminum sculpture on the moon to memorialize fallen astronauts. In 1971, that number was 14. There's also a plaque bearing their names.

21. Squirrels have actually been known to adopt another squirrel's baby if the parent dies.

22. Monkey brains are considered a delicacy in parts of South Asia, Africa, and China.They're considered an easily digestible substance often given to children, and there are even entire cookbooks dedicated to how to cook them.

23. The Satere-Mawe Indians initiate their boys at the age of 13 by making them wear gloves made of bullet ants for 10 minutes. They are repeatedly bitten, which is incredibly painful, but must not cry out if they want to be declared a man.

24. Octopuses will actually break off a limb as part of a fight to impress a mate or to get away from a predator. They will also eat their own arms once in a while, which some scientists believe may be due to a disease of some sort.

25. When flying in a flock, Flamingos can fly as fast as 35 miles (55 km) per hour. They may seem clumsy in flight, however, because this is because their long necks stretch out in front of their bodies, and their long legs dangle well past their short tails.

26. In California, there's a law that prohibits a vehicle without a driver to exceed 60 miles (97 km) per hour. Companies like Google who make autonomous cars have the technology to make them go much faster but must limit them based on this law.

27. There is an app that exists called 'Photo Math', that solves any math equation you can point your phone at.

28. Lobsters have some really weird anatomy. Their brains are in their throats, their nervous systems are in their abdomens, their teeth are in their stomachs, and their kidneys are in their heads.

29. The Carrot House in Warsaw is the world's tiniest house measuring only 92 centimeters at its narrowest point and 152 centimeters at its widest.

30. Africam is a website that brings you live, 24/7 video feed of protected areas of southern Africa. You can watch elephants, giraffes, zebras, hyenas and all kinds of species of wildlife living there.
31. There is a 1966 Volvo with more than 3 million miles on it.
32. Horror movie soundtracks sometimes include infrasound, which is sound below the range of human hearing. Even though we can't hear it, we can still feel it, and infrasound has been shown to induce anxiety, heart palpitations, and even shivering.
33. In Japan, you can hire a handsome man to show up at your office and watch sad videos with you until you cry and then wipe away your tears for you.
34. Charles Baldwin, designer of the international biohazard symbol, said regarding his design, we wanted to create something that was memorable but meaningless so that we could educate people as to what it means.
35. The total cost of climbing Mount Everest, to pay for 'Sherpas', supplies and permits, is between $60,000 and $120,000.
36. According to the Guinness World Records, as of 2015, the world record for long distance archery is held by a paralympic, armless archer, Matt Stutzman.
37. There is a ten-year-old girl named Esther Okade who is already enrolled in university and has the highest exam scores in her class. She mastered algebra at the age of four.
38. The rarest wild cat in the world is the Bornean Bay Cat. Only 12 have ever been captured and studied between the years of 1874 and 2002. That's one every 10 years.
39. Shani Shingnapur is a small village in India with 300 buildings, all of which have no doors in their doorways. These people leave their homes, businesses, and schools open at all times under the belief that if anyone does anything dishonest, that they will face seven years bad luck.
40. In 1883, the body of a bear and a man named Frank Devereaux were found dead side-by-side with the ground around them thrashed. It's believed that the man and bear fought to the death.

41. There are over 500 hundred different ways to cook potatoes. In fact, a recipe book on it was put together by former Soviet leader Mikhail Gorbachev's wife and was gifted to Britain. It now sits in the British foreign office.

42. There is a bottle of vodka that costs 3.75 million U.S. dollars, and it's filtered through sand made from crushed diamonds and gems.

43. A study concluded by the Journal of Positive Psychology concluded that two-thirds of humans have no idea what they're good at and what their strengths are.

44. In 2014, Beyonce made about $3.65 U.S. every second.

45. The Pixar team came up with the concepts of "Wall-E", "A Bug's Life", "Monsters Inc.", and "Finding Nemo" all over a lunch-break in 1994.

46. There is a floating stage in Singapore that sits above the water that can bear the weight of 9,000 people. It's used as a soccer field, concert stage, and place of celebration.

47. The world's tallest man Bao Xishun, used his long arms reaching 1.06 meters to remove plastic from the stomachs of two dolphins, which ultimately saved their lives after trainers tried numerous other methods.

48. When Julius Caesar first discovered giraffes, he named them camelopards, since they reminded him of both camels and leopards.

49. British banking giant HSBC admitted to laundering billions of dollars for Colombian and Mexican drug cartels and violating a host of important banking laws. But, somehow, there were no criminal charges and no one went to jail.

50. You can't usually smell your own house or perfume because of the survival instinct called "olfactory adaptation". The brain is always looking for new, unusual, or changing smells as a sign of possible danger. So, it ignores smells that it has become familiar with.

51. There is a company called Hoxton Street Monster Supplies that sells salt made from real human tears, and disturbingly there are

four kinds, harvested from different moments. Sneezing, chopping onions, laughter and anger.

52. An Australian man named Don Ritchie lives across the street from the most famous suicide spot in Australia; a cliff known as The Gap. He, alone, has prevented around 160 suicides in his 50 years of living there by striking up a conversation with people contemplating suicide by inviting them into his house for tea.

53. For the past 15 years, a Bulgarian man named Dobri Dobrev has walked up to 25 kilometers every single day to beg for money for orphanages that are unable to pay their bills. He turned 101 in July of this year.

54. An adopted man in Michigan named Steve Flaig searched for his birth mother for four years before finally discovering in 2007 that she worked at the same Lowe's store that he worked at. Amazingly neither of them knew.

55. A moment is actually a medieval unit of time equal to 90 seconds. There are 40 moments in an hour.

56. The Queen of England's portrait has been on enough International money to make a progressive timeline of her aging.

57. An Abu-Dhabi oil sheik named Hamad Bin Hamdan Al Nahyan carved his name in the desert in letters that are over 1,000 meters long.

58. Istanbul has a vending machine that releases food and water for stray dogs in exchange for recyclable bottles.

59. The first animal to ever ask an existential question was from a parrot named Alex. He asked what color he was, and learned that he was gray.

60. In January 1961 the U.S. Air Force accidentally dropped two nuclear bombs in Goldsboro North Carolina when a bomber broke in half in the air. Fortunately, the bomb didn't go off but if it did it would've caused more destruction than Hiroshima and Nagasaki.

61. People who are in love can actually synchronize their heartbeats just by gazing into each others' eyes.

62. Exercising increases productivity. Having a regular exercise routine can make you happier, smarter and more energetic and thus last longer throughout the day.

63. In 2009 archaeologists discovered the fossils of a primitive species of crocodiles that actually galloped. They lived 100 million years ago, walked with the dinosaurs and sometimes even ate them.

64. Approximately 50% of Asians have trouble metabolizing alcohol because they're missing a liver enzyme that's needed to process it.

65. England's Big Ben is actually leaning to the northwest by .26 degrees, putting it out of alignment at its highest point by 1.6 feet. It was discovered when Transport for London commissioned a report, that the London clay on which the tower was built on is drying out, causing the lean.

66. In 1930, the planet Pluto was named by an 11-year-old named Venetia Burney. She suggested the name Pluto to her grandfather, who in turn suggested it to a friend who happened to be an astronomy professor at Oxford University. He was also one of the leaders in the worldwide effort to produce an astrographic chart.

67. According to a study done in 2001 by Diane Reese of the Osborn Laboratory of Marine Sciences at the New York Aquarium, dolphins actually recognize themselves and notice changes in their appearance when looking in a mirror. Prior to this research, only higher primates, such as humans and chimpanzees had demonstrated self-recognition in mirrors.

68. Researchers at the University of Montreal have concluded that everyone has the potential ability to be a good singer. It's a developed skill that gets better with practice and worse by lack of use.

69. There's an infrared device that exists that detects the locations of medical patients' veins and projects them onto the skin.

70. The Keikyu Aburatsubo Marine Park in Japan has tiny holes in the otter enclosure which allows visitors to shake hands with these animals.
71. A group of pandas is known as an embarrassment.
72. In 1948 the committee responsible for awarding the Nobel Peace Prize chose no one, stating there was no suitable living candidate, mostly as a tribute to Mahatma Gandhi who was assassinated earlier that year.
73. The word "BAE" which is popular in North American society is actually the Danish word for poop.
74. You can tell identical twin babies apart by their navels since the navel is a scar and isn't caused by genetics.
75. Allen Gans holds the world record for the longest person as an ice-cream man. He's been serving ice cream since 1947 in the greater Boston area and knows 90 % of his customers by name.
76. The Nasir Almoque Mosque in Iran is known for its incredible stained glass windows. When the morning sunlight shines through the windows, the interior of the mosque reflects the windows like a kaleidoscope.
77. In 1995 NASA scientists experimented on spiders to see how drugs like LSD, marijuana, caffeine, and peyote would affect them. The results showed that spiders would spin webs differently depending on the type of drug that they were given. The more toxic the drug, the less organized their webs were.
78. Soviet diplomat Vyacheslav Molotov is thought to be the only man to ever shake hands with Stalin, Lenin, Hitler, Himmler, Goering, Roosevelt, and Churchill and is also the inspiration behind the term Molotov cocktail.
79. The Wright brothers only ever flew together once, in 1910. This is because their father feared losing both sons in an airplane accident, so he gave them special permission just that one time.
80. Psychopaths are only capable of perceiving the positive consequences for their actions as opposed to any negative ones.
81. When you yawn and stretch at the time, you are "pandiculating."

82. Tupac danced ballet in high school and ended up portraying the Mouse King in a production of The Nutcracker.

83. Babies are born without kneecaps. They don't appear until the child reaches 2-6 years of age.

84. Arnold Schonberg suffered from triskaidekaphobia, the fear of the number 13. He died at 13 minutes from midnight on Friday the 13th.

85. Actor Sean Bean is so terrified of flying that during the filming of Lord of the Rings while shooting in remote mountain locations, he traveled via sky lift and walked the remainder of the journey all in full costume.

86. There are fireworks that can be set off in daylight by using colored smoke.

87. That dark band that you can see between the primary and secondary bows of a rainbow has a name. It's been referred to as Alexander's band or Alexander's dark band after Alexander of Aphrodisiacs first described it in 200 AD.

88. The Chinese giant salamander is the world's largest living amphibian and can grow up to six feet (1.8 meters) long and can weigh as much as 110 pounds (500 kg).

89. Watermelon is made up of 92% water. It's actually an excellent choice to stay hydrated and is low in calories.

90. It's possible for a poisonous snake, after being decapitated for hours, to bite and inject venom and still kill you. According to Steven Beaupre, a biology professor at the University of Arkansas, snakes are well-known for retaining reflexes after death. For venomous snakes like cobras and rattlesnakes, biting is one of those reflexes.

91. In the 15 and 1600s, women who were seen gossiping, riotous, or troublesome were made to wear scold's bridle, also known as branks, as punishment. Disturbingly, it was made of an iron frame that encased the head, and at the front was a bridle or bit, like a horse, that extended into the mouth and held down the tongue with a spiked plate. It literally made it impossible to speak, so it was basically a muzzle for a woman.

92. After Abraham Lincoln was assassinated his body was taken on a two-week, 1,600-mile (2500 km) tour via train. He was accompanied by the body of his son, William Wallace Lincoln, who had died of typhoid fever at the age of only 11, and buried in the DC area of 1862. The train made a tour through 400 train stations, and viewings were arranged where his body was on display for mourners.

93. In 2006, Michigan woman Lynn Sterling tried to sell a mummified human skeleton on eBay. eBay removed the posting because it violated their policy against selling human remains.

94. It's possible for cats and dogs to be allergic to human dander. Dander is made up of tiny cells shed from hair, fur, or feathers. And though you mostly hear it in relation to pets, humans produce it too.

95. The mantis shrimp can punch with a speed equal to a bullet, fifty times that of a blink of an eye. In fact, a blow from a mantis shrimp can easily break through the shell of a crab or mollusk.

96. Until 1987, all surgeries performed on infants were done without anesthesia, under the belief that infants were not capable of feeling pain.

97. In 2012 a man sued Pepsi after he found a mouse in his Mountain Dew. However, Pepsi fought and won the case, proving that any mouse would have dissolved inside a can of Mountain Dew after 30 days and that this can was purchased 74 days after being manufactured.

98. Railroad tycoon George Pullman's family were so worried that former employees would desecrate his corpse after death that they buried him at night in a pit 2.4 meters deep under layers of steel reinforced concrete in a lead-lined casket.

99. Elephants can use the skin folds on their backs to crush mosquitos.

100. There is a doctor in Nepal named Sanduk Ruit who has restored vision to over 100,000 people in the developing world.

101. In the average lifetime, a person will walk the equivalent of 5 times around the equator.

102. A research paper from 2013 concluded that Harry Potter fans tend to be more open to diversity, politically tolerant, less authoritarian, and less likely to support the use of deadly force or torture.
103. You can be criminally prosecuted for making death threats written entirely in emoji.
104. If you were to commit suicide in Japan by either jumping in front of a train or killing yourself in your apartment building, the train or building company will actually sue your family for clean-up fees, loss of income, and negative publicity brought upon them by your suicide.
105. James Cameron was actually homeless when he wrote 'The Terminator' and sold the rights to it for only one dollar on the condition that he could direct it.
106. -40 Celsius and -40 Fahrenheit are the same temperature.
107. A company by the name of Vestergaard Frandsen, in Europe, launched a LifeStraw in 2006, which makes contaminated water safe to drink. Users simply just have to suck up the contaminated water through it as if they were any other regular straw. Without using batteries or chemicals, it removes 99.9% of parasites, 99.9999% of viruses and provides one person with an entire year's worth of drinking water for only $20.00.
108. One of the ingredients needed to make dynamite is peanuts.
109. In Dubai, there's a weight loss competition called 'Your Child In Gold'. The campaign is aimed at early obesity and winners get 90 pounds (40 kilograms) in gold.
110. The pet rock became so popular when it came out that within the first six months of its release, Gary Doll the inventor earned $15 million.
111. While you sleep you can't smell anything, even really bad or potent smells.
112. In 1963 Alfred Heineken designed the 'Heineken World Bottle', a brick that holds beer that can be used to build houses. Unfortunately, the project never came into fruition and the

Heineken estate and museum are the only two places in the entire world with a beer brick wall.

113. The Gippsland Lakes in Victoria, Australia glows in the dark. The light is created by a chemical reaction called bioluminescence when naturally occurring microorganisms in the water are disturbed.

114. In 2012, Healthpoint Biotherapeutics, of Fort Worth, Texas, developed a portable, spray-on skin, that can heal severe wounds much faster. The spray-on skin is actually made up of skin cells and suspended in a mixture of different types of proteins.

115. Andre the Giant died on the night of January 27th, 1993 in a hotel room in Paris. Coincidentally, he was in Paris to attend his father's funeral.

116. The longest mathematical proof in history is 15,000 pages long, involved more than 100 mathematicians, and took over 30 years to complete.

117. Some of the largest spider webs in the world are built by the Anelosimus Eximius; a breed of social spider that works together in a community. Over 50,000 spiders can live on one web until they eventually outgrow it and have to form new colonies.

118. Apples originated in Kazakhstan, and wild apples can taste like roses, strawberries, popcorn, anise, and many other flavors. In fact, 90% of modern apples can be traced back to two trees.

119. Rotterdam, in the Netherlands, is getting a floating forest. They're taking 20 trees that have been removed for development and placing them in boats throughout the waterfront.

120. Yellow snow isn't the only snow you shouldn't eat. According to a new study published in the Journal of Environmental Science Processes and Impacts, all snow can be harmful because it attracts particles from car exhaust fumes like a magnet.

121. Instead of its Gross National Product, Bhutan measures its development and prosperity by its Gross National Happiness. It's been doing this since 1971 and is the only country to do so.

122. There is an English law called right to light that allows long-standing owners of buildings that receive natural daylight for at least 20 years, to forbid any construction that would block the windows and deprive them of that light.

123. Greek statues aren't actually white like we thought they were. Ultraviolet light has revealed that they were once originally brightly painted, but after thousands of years, the paint's wore away to show the statues as we know them today.

124. Vikings never actually wore horned helmets. The only helmet that was discovered to be a Viking heritage shows a rounded iron cap and no horns whatsoever.

125. In 1950, almost the entire Soviet hockey team died in a plane crash. The team's manager was Vasily Stalin, son of Joseph Stalin. He was afraid of his father's reaction to the crash and recruited a whole team immediately and surprisingly, his father never knew the difference.

126. You can rent the entire country of Liechtenstein for 70,000 dollars a night. In fact, Snoop Dogg once tried to do that in 2011 for a video shoot but the country said no primarily because he just didn't give them enough notice.

127. Australia literally lost a prime minister Harold Holt, on December 17th of 1967, who went for a swim and just never came back.

128. High atmospheric pressure affects the bubbles in your coffee. Therefore, if bubbles are closer to the center, you can expect it to rain or have other stormy weather.

129. Elephants remember and mourn their loved ones like us, sometimes years after their death.

130. In 1999 a woman named Penny Brown saved a little boy, Kevin Stefan's life by giving him CPR after he was hit in the chest with a baseball bat. However, just seven years later, he ended up saving her from choking to death by giving her the Heimlich maneuver.

131. There is a cryptid that's believed to exist in the Gobi Desert called the Mongolian Death Worm. It can grow up to 1.5 meters long and kills its prey with electric shocks from its eyes.

132. In 2013 a bank worker in Germany fell asleep on his keyboard's number-two button causing him to transfer 222,222,222 euros on a transfer that should have been worth only 62 euros. Interestingly his coworker was the one fired for not spotting the error.

133. Users upload an average of 350 million photos to Facebook every day and in total have uploaded more than 250 billion photos to date.

134. The role of Captain Jack Sparrow was originally offered to Jim Carrey but he turned it down for the role of Bruce Almighty.

135. According to neuroscientist Glen Jeffrey, who investigates vision at the University College London, the eye color of reindeer changes depending on the time of year. In the summer, they actually turn golden, reflecting more light through the retina, which helps them deal with the almost continuous Arctic summer daylight. In the winter however, they turn a deep blue to help them deal with the almost continuous winter darkness.

136. There's a Sign Post Forest just outside of Watson Lake, Yukon. It was started in 1942 when a soldier named Carl K. Lindley was injured while working on the Alcan Highway. He was taken to the Army air station in Watson Lake to recuperate. While he was there he was homesick, so he decided to put up a sign of Danville, Illinois, his hometown. Tourists continued the tradition, and there are currently 72,000 signs from around the world.

137. Since the first nuclear test explosion on July 16th, 1945, at least eight nations have detonated 2,054 nuclear test explosions at dozens of test sites around the world.

138. There's something that exists called elimination communication where, instead of using diapers, the parent learns to use timing, signals, and cues to know when their baby needs to pee or poo.

139. Jackrabbits are actually hares, not rabbits. They can reach speeds of 40 miles (64 km) per hour and jump as high as 10 feet (3 meters) in the air.

140. The Lehe Ledu Wildlife Zoo in Chongqing, China, put the people visiting the zoo in cages instead of the animals. The cages are

stalked by lions and tigers, so the guests are warned to keep their fingers and hands inside the cage at all times.

141. The unborn babies of a female sea louse actually chew their way out of the mother's insides to be born.

142. A 63-year-old Tasmanian woman gave birth to her first baby in August of 2016, making her Australia's oldest new mother.

143. According to a report from the Center for Disease Control and Prevention's National Center for Health Statistics, American men now weigh, on average, 196 pounds (89 kg) on average, 15 pounds (7 kg) more than 20 years ago, and women weigh 168 pounds (76 kg), which is 16 pounds (7 kg) more than 20 years ago.

144. There's a flower called the corpse flower, which is called that because it smells like putrefying and decaying flesh, which only blooms every seven to 10 years.

145. According to a study done in 2012 by Japanese researcher Hiroshi Nittono, looking at images of cute animals like puppies and pandas at work not only improve your mood but also boosts your attention to detail and overall performance.

146. An Iowa artist named Patrick Acton built a complete model of Hogwarts out of six hundred and two thousand matchsticks held together by almost 60 liters of wood glue.

147. Sugar gliders are such social creatures that if they're deprived of social interaction they can actually become depressed and die.

148. In the Middle Ages, doctors believed that farting into jars and sniffing them, would prevent death or more specifically the black death plague which they called therapeutic stink.

149. The richest woman in Germany Susanne Klatten met her husband while she was working in an internship for BMW under a fake name. In the 1980s he had no idea who she actually was until she was sure about the relationship when she revealed herself.

150. There are approximately 10 quintillion insects on the planet. That's 10 with 18 zeros behind it or roughly 200 million insects per human.

151. In 1992, thousands of plastic yellow ducks broke free from a cargo ship in the middle of the Pacific Ocean, and for the past 23 years, these ducks have since turned up in locations all over the world, and have even been used to track ocean currents.
152. Research conducted at the University of Stanford concluded that a racially diverse group has the ability to solve problems more effectively than a group with only one race in it.
153. If you watch any classic Clint Eastwood film, you will often see his character smoking like Dirty Harry, despite the fact that Clint never smoked habitually in real life, and actually practiced healthy dieting and meditation since his youth.
154. In South Korea, children under 17 are blocked from playing online games past midnight, which is monitored by their KSSN, the Korean Social Security Number.
155. On April Fool's Day in 1989, billionaire Richard Branson designed a hot air balloon to look like a UFO and hired a dwarf in an ET costume to come out and scare whoever was near it when it landed.
156. The band Blink-182 incorporated under the name Pennywise Poo Poo Butt Inc so that their accountants, managers, and attorneys would have to say that when doing business.
157. When James Bond actor, Daniel Craig first ran off with his current wife Rachel Weisz in 2010, he actually had a fiancée at the time. And when she found out, she spent a million dollars on his credit line in revenge.
158. Robert Hubbard was executed in 1666 for starting the great fire of London by claiming he threw a firebomb through a bakery window. However, this was despite the fact that he was heavily crippled, the bakery had no windows, and it was proved at his trial that he wasn't even in the country at the time.
159. Jennifer Lopez's common nickname in parts of Hong Kong and China is Lord of Butt.
160. Pharrell Williams was fired from three separate McDonald's restaurants when he was 17 for being lazy and stealing McNuggets.

161. Every December 25th, the inhabitants of the Chumbivilcas Province in Peru celebrate Takanakuy. This is where men settle grudges from the past year by calling each other out and having a fistfight. Then everybody goes drinking to numb the pain and move on to a new year.

162. There exists a set of 19 questions among doctors such as "do we have the right patient" and "what operation are we performing" known as the "safe surgery checklist" which has been proven to reduce surgical deaths by more than 40 percent.

163. 65% of smartphone users download zero apps per month.

164. The great pyramids in Egypt were actually shiny like glass at one point 4,000 years ago. Craftsmen were tasked to polish the stone surfaces to perfection.

165. In 2010, Mattel made and sold Wonder Woman's invisible jet as a collectible. The package was an empty plastic shell with nothing inside and the packaging had weights to give the illusion that there was actually something inside, and people bought this.

166. Actor Don Johnson once asked famed journalist Hunter S. Thompson what is the sound of one hand clapping. Hunter S. Thompson answered by reaching up and slapping Johnson upside the head.

167. Blind people forget many memories since they don't have visual imagery and can't look at pictures to reminisce. A 3D printing company known as Touchable Memories prints 3D objects from old photos so that the blind can touch them, feel, and relive their cherished moments like never before.

168. Jamaica, Colombia, and Saint Lucia are the only countries in the world where a boss is more likely to be a woman than a man.

169. Believe it or not, you can determine the temperature outside by counting the chirps made by crickets. According to the Farmer's Almanac, to convert cricket chirps to degrees celsius, you count the number of chirps in 25 seconds, divide by three, then add four to get the temperature.

170. There's something called a moonbow or lunar rainbow that's a rainbow that can be seen at night and happens very rarely. In

order for this to happen, a full moon is needed, it must be raining opposite to the moon, the sky must be dark, and the moon must be less than 42 degrees high.

171. The longest solar eclipse in the 21st century lasted six minutes and 39 seconds, and it won't be surpassed in duration until the eclipse of June 13, 2132.

172. Venus and Uranus are the only planets that rotate clockwise. The other six planets in the solar system rotate counterclockwise.

173. Pope Francis broke a record when he hit one million Instagram followers within 12 hours of starting the account. The previous record was set by David Beckham at one million within 24 hours. He christened the account on a Saturday with a photo of him kneeling in prayer with an accompanying message that said, "Pray for me," in nine languages.

174. Before Samuel L. Jackson became a movie star, he was Bill Cosby's camera stand-in 'On The Cosby Show'.

175. Leonardo da Vinci was dyslexic. Also strangely, not because of his dyslexia, he chose to write all of his notes to himself backward in mirror writing, meaning that you can only read them in the reflection of a mirror. However notes that he wrote to other people, he wrote in a normal direction.

176. A college student in 1979 only had to work about 182 hours per year in order to pay for tuition. The average student in 2013 had to work over 991.

177. Penguin One, an organic chemical compound, got its name from the fact that its molecular structure resembles a penguin.

178. The heaviest human ever recorded was Jon Minnoch and weighed 1,400 pounds (635 kg). He later lost approximately 924 pounds (419 kg), the largest human weight loss ever documented.

179. The idea for the film 'The Human Centipede' came from a joke made by the writer/director Tom Six on how child molesters should be punished.

180. During the late 1800's, a baboon named Jack was employed by the railroad in Cape Town, South Africa as a signalman. He never once made a mistake and worked for the railroad until his death.

181. Scientists have begun arguing that we may actually have more than five basic senses including magnetoception, the ability to detect magnetic fields and Chronoception, the sense of time passing.

182. In 1898 Bayer introduced diacetylmorphine, marketed as a cure for morphine addiction and cough suppressant. Today that drug is better known by the name heroin.

183. In the 1930s an Argentinean engineer named Juan Vilar created a rain-making machine and successfully made it rain in several places at once. He then disappeared without a trace.

184. Marvel's The Avengers movie caused shawarma sales to skyrocket nationwide in America in 2012, purely because of an extra scene in which Thor, Captain America, Bruce Banner, and the rest of the heroic clan are quietly enjoying shawarma after casually saving the world.

185. The most densely populated island on the planet is Santa Cruz del Islote, off the coast of Colombia. It measures only about 0.012 kilometers but is home to over 12,000 people.

186. A biotech startup has managed to print 3D rhino horns that are genetically similar to a real horn. The best thing about it is the company plans to flood Chinese and Vietnamese markets, where the demand is high, and bring down the price, and thus, demands.

187. The movie Straight Outta Compton didn't play in Compton because there are no theaters there.

188. A man in the United Kingdom was so fed up that his city wasn't repairing potholes he went and spray painted penises on them earning him the nickname "Wanksy."

189. There is a natural rock formation off the coast of Iceland that looks like a giant elephant.

190. Donald Trump was actually the inspiration for the character Biff Tanned in the Back to the Future trilogy.

191. There is a bookstore in Australia where books are wrapped in paper with short descriptions so that no one can judge a book by its cover.

192. In Albania, nodding your head means no, and shaking your head means yes.

193. A human taste bud has an average lifespan of seven to 10 days. Taste bud cells undergo continual turnover, even into adulthood, but taste buds in rats last from two days to over three weeks.

194. There were over 13 couples celebrating their honeymoon on the Titanic, however, none of them survived upon impact and the subsequent sinking of the boat.

195. Dogs love the herb anise the same way that cats love catnip. In fact, anise is the scent of the artificial rabbit that is used in greyhound races to get the dogs to run.

196. The hardest bone in the human body is the jawbone. Also known as the mandible, it's also the largest and strongest bone in the human face.

197. Believe it or not, you consume 1/10th of a calorie by licking a U.S. stamp, but if you were to lick a stamp in Britain, it's 5.9 calories per lick and the adhesive on a larger commemorative or special British stamp contains a whopping 14.5 calories.

198. Camels actually have three eyelids to protect their eyes from blowing sand. The upper and lower eyelids have eyelashes, however, there's a third one that's a thin membrane that they can see through even in a sandstorm.

199. Your sense of smell and taste begin to improve dramatically within 48 hours of quitting smoking.

200. Potatoes have almost all the nutrients that humans need to survive. To prove this, the executive director from the Washington State Potato Commission, ate nothing but potatoes for 60 days and was just fine.

201. Caromont Farms, in Esmont, Virginia, posted a message on its Facebook page earlier this year, looking for volunteers to snuggle with its baby goats. Not surprisingly, the signup list filled up immediately.

202. After its tourism sector boomed, Kazakhstan's foreign minister thanked Sacha Baron Cohen back in 2012 for the release of Borat after the country saw a 10 times increase in issued visas.

203. In 2014, a woman named Nancy Cohen was moved into a nursing home. Her relocated cat, Cleo, showed up two weeks later, even though she had never been there before. She started hanging out on benches until somebody noticed her, and now they live together at the facility.

204. The Taxi Fabric Project in Mumbai, India lets upcoming designers reupholster and completely transform taxi cab interiors.

205. There is a unique tree near Piemonte, Italy called The Double Tree of Casorzo. It's actually two trees in one, a cherry tree growing on top of a mulberry tree.

206. According to Daniel J. Buysse, a psychiatrist at the University of Pittsburgh Medical Center, about two percent of the population are considered the sleepless elite. This means that they are night owls and early birds simultaneously.

207. When Neuroscientist James Fallon was studying the brains of psychopathic killers, he scanned his own brain as a control, only to discover that he himself was a psychopath. When he told his friends and family, the universal response was "That explains a lot."

208. Argentine ants have a worldwide mega-colony. In fact, if they got on an airplane and traveled to a different continent, they would actually be welcomed by a foreign branch of the colony.

209. A study once found that, while sober, rats prefer silence, but on cocaine, they prefer jazz.

210. In the 1930s, two psychologists adopted a baby chimp and tried to raise her as their own child alongside their real infant son, Donald, to see if it caused the chimp to learn human behavior. They stopped the experiment after nine months because their son actually started behaving more like the chimp.

211. Gun laws in Japan are so strict that even when a police officer killed himself with one once, he was posthumously charged with breaking the law.

212. Ravens are one of the smartest animals on earth. They actually try to hide their food from each other but are only sometimes successful because they're all so smart.

213. Various studies have shown that coffee prevents cancer, reduces the risk of diabetes, and can improve overall health.

214. John F. Kennedy's grandmother, Mary Josephine Fitzgerald, not only outlived her grandson, but she was never told about his assassination.

215. In the early 1930s, Warner Brothers began producing animated shorts specifically for the purpose of promoting music owned by the company. They were called Looney Tunes.

216. When Google first announced Gmail on April 1st with an unbelievable one gig of free storage, back in 2004, which at the time seemed impossible with Hotmail only offering 2 megabytes, people thought that it was an April Fool's Day joke.

217. Believe it or not, outer space is only an hour away if you could drive a car straight into the sky at 96 kilometers an hour or 60 miles an hour.

218. In the early 1800s, Napoleon demanded a method of communication that would not require light or sound. It was called night writing and was developed as a tactile military code. Night writing became the basis for braille.

219. Niccolo Paganini, regarded by many people to be the greatest violin virtuoso of all time, was so good that in the early 1800s, people began to question if he had sold his soul to the devil for his talent. He was actually forced to publish his mother's letters to him in order to prove that he had human parents.

220. At one point during the 1985 Geneva Summit, Reagan and Gorbachev agreed to pause the Cold War in case of an alien invasion.

221. A poisonous lagoon at the quarry in Buxton, England was dyed black for safety. The previous beautiful, azure blue watercolor was so inviting that the signs did not keep swimmers out.

222. The world's deepest, darkest, oldest, and quietest motel room is 230 feet (70 meter) underground, at Grand Canyon Caverns in a 65,000,000-year-old cave.
223. Knowledge of silk production was thought to be very valuable and the Chinese kept it a secret for over 3,000 years. In fact, it was so secret that anyone who revealed it was sentenced to death by imperial decrees.
224. A Japanese gymnast named Shun Fujimoto once broke his knee at the Olympics in 1976 but didn't tell anybody and performed miraculously despite his injury, even winning his team a gold medal.
225. There's a town in Australia where the entire town, 200-plus people live underground in abandoned opal mines. Residents here have electricity and plumbing and have been known to find vast amounts of opal when renovating.
226. Artist Susan Beatrice recycles old watch parts and turns them into intricate steampunk sculptures.
227. George Hotz, then 17 years old, was the first to unlock a first-generation iPhone and sold the iPhone for a Nissan 350Z and three locked phones.
228. There's a pepper, grown in Japan, known as the "Shishito pepper". Only one out of every 10 is spicy, and there's no way to know which one beforehand.
229. There's a mental disorder called maladaptive daydreaming, which causes people to excessively daydream to escape reality as a defense mechanism due to trauma, usually from abuse.
230. More people have died from selfies than shark attacks.
231. Treadmills were actually created to punish English prisoners in 1818.
232. Dr. Duncan MacDougall, Haverhill, once attempted to prove that the human soul had weight by placing dying patients on a giant scale at the exact moment of death. Believe it or not, at the exact moment of death, there was a slight decrease in weight.

233. Experiences that you have throughout your life leave chemical markers on your DNA, essentially ingraining superficial experiences into your descendants.

234. Photographer Chompoo Baritone created a photo series that aims at exposing the truth by mocking Instagram users who prop and filter their lives to make them seem more amazing than they really are.

235. There is a phenomenon that exists called cellular memory. It occurs when organ transplant recipients experience the same thoughts and cravings as their organ donors.

236. There is a fish that exists called the Blue Lingcod that has blue flesh. When it's cooked the blue color vanishes completely.

237. On July 5, 1996, the first mammal ever was successfully cloned. Dolly the sheep was cloned from an adult cell at the Roslin Institute in Scotland. She was named after Dolly Parton because she was cloned from a mammary cell.

238. Mosquitoes can detect carbon dioxide from 75 feet away. In fact, that's how they find their victims.

239. A galactic year, also known as a cosmic year is the duration of a complete rotation of the Milky Way, which is approximately 200 million terrestrial years.

240. The human aorta is the largest artery in the human body and is about the size of a garden hose.

241. There is a dog breed called Basenji that doesn't have the ability to bark. It can produce a yodeling howl sound though. It's a small to medium sized, square-shaped animal that is believed to be bred intentionally without the ability to bark.

242. In 2008, the Japanese created a silicon toy called Mugen Puti Puti designed to mimic the sensation of popping bubble wrap for an infinite number of times.

243. Mexican shamans began to use Coca-Cola in their religious rituals to heal worshipers. When Pepsi discovered this, they offered commissions to Shamans for using Pepsi instead.

244. Keiko, the orca who starred in Free Willy, was released into the wild in July of 2002 in Iceland after being in captivity for 23 years.

A few weeks after his release he showed up at a Norwegian inlet from the sea, looking to make human contact and gave children rides on his back.

245. If you're looking for a job, the application and resume are not nearly as important as a reference. In fact, knowing someone who works at the company increases your chances of getting an interview and makes you 40% more likely to get the job over someone with a fancier resume.

246. Jim Wenqi, a blind man, and Jia Haixia a double amputee, together planted 10,000 trees in Yeli Village located in Northern China and plan on planting another 10,000.

247. According to the world drug report of 2014, Scotland had the highest rate of cocaine use in the world.

248. While on his deathbed in 1778, French philosopher Voltaire was asked to renounce Satan to which he replied: "Now is not the time to be making new enemies" which are thought to be his last words.

249. Some of the crew working on 'American Horror Story Freak Show' would have to actually leave set at times because 'Twisty the Clown' was so scary while others would complain of nightmares after filming.

250. Famed writer H.G. Wells' last words on his deathbed in 1946 were "Go away, I'm all right."

251. Studies in the UK for automotive accidents concluded that short female drivers who sit close to the steering wheel are the most likely to be killed by an airbag.

252. McDonald's in Hong Kong will soon host cheap "McWeddings" for couples at a cost of around $1,200 and will actually provide food, drink, and an apple pie for 50 people.

253. A study conducted in 2013 by the BBC found that 56% of pilots fell asleep while flying and 29% had woken up to find that the copilot was also asleep.

254. A German engineering company has created the world's first-rope free elevator system that uses a magnetic technology

which allows elevators to travel sideways as well as up and down.

255. Economics professors at Emory University found that those who spend below average on their weddings and on their wedding rings have lower divorce rates.

256. There is only one species of warm-blooded fish on Earth, the Opah.

257. Pixar spent three years studying the physics of curly hair in order to correctly render Merida's hair in Brave.

258. If you come across a stranded dolphin, do not help it back into the water. More often than not, they beach themselves purposely because they are sick or injured, and are trying to avoid drowning.

259. In 1888 a pigeon keeper and a beekeeper challenged each other's creatures to a 3.5 mile (5.6 kilometer) organized race in Germany. The bee won by 25 seconds.

260. When the Confederate Army was low on gun powder, bat caves were raided for poop. Bat poop contains high nitrate content which is a key ingredient for the production of gunpowder.

261. In 1991, drug lord Pablo Escobar got to build his own prison known as La Cathedral. It featured a soccer field, a giant dollhouse, a bar, a Jacuzzi, and a waterfall. It's where he stayed for only one year and one month after he was caught torturing his guests.

262. Wild chimpanzees look both ways before crossing the road. The National Museum of Natural History in Paris began studying their vigilance and found that 57% of the time, they would run across the road to be extra safe.

263. Astronomers have discovered the largest known diamond in the universe is a star named Lucy that is ten trillion, billion karats. This white dwarf has a carbon interior that crystallized as it cooled which formed a giant diamond in the sky. Scientists couldn't resist naming it after The Beatles' song 'Lucy in the Sky with Diamonds'.

264. In 2013, a dog named Killian saved a baby boy from an abusive babysitter when he alerted his owners by growling and standing between the baby and the sitter whenever she was present. The parents later recorded the abuse and the sitter was convicted.

265. Panama is the only place in the world where one can see the sunrise on the Pacific Ocean, and set on the Atlantic.

266. In 1905, 11-year-old Frank Epperson from the San Francisco Bay area invented the popsicle by accident. He left his sugary soda powder that he mixed with water outside overnight and the next morning, it was frozen. He originally named it the eppsicle, but the name was eventually changed to popsicle.

267. There's a phobia called allodoxaphobia that's actually the fear of people's opinions. People with this live in constant fear and anxiety of hearing other people's opinions of them.

268. A group of flamingos is called a flamboyance of flamingos.

269. In 1922, Charles Osborne got a case of the hiccups that lasted until 1990. He was hiccuping 40 times a minute for 68 years and possibly the weirdest thing is that when it stopped, it stopped for unknown reasons.

270. The New York Presbyterian Morgan Stanley Children's Hospital has a CT scan room that has been turned into a pirate-themed island. Children enter the room by walking on a plank and then lay on a boat-shaped table.

271. Steven Jay Russell escaped four times from prison. The first time, he simply walked out. Upon recapture, Russell lowered and paid his bail by pretending to be a judge, escaped his next capture by impersonating a doctor, and did so again by then faking his death. Eventually, he received a 144-year sentence that he is still currently serving.

272. In 2010, musician Dave Grohl was admitted into a hospital due to a drug overdose. The drug was that he had actually consumed too much caffeine from coffee while recording a new album.

273. Studies conducted by the University of Toronto concluded that the more that one trusts people, the better they are at spotting liars.

274. A Japanese soldier was stranded on an island for 30 years after the Second World War had ended. He continued to stand his post in uniform until his commander came to the island to personally dismiss him in 1974.

275. In 1978, Soviet geologists found a family of six that survived in the middle of Serbia who hadn't seen another human since 1936.

276. Pumbaa was the first-ever character to fart in a Disney movie.

277. Purple is known as a royal color because back when they relied on only natural dyes purple came from sea snails and it was the hardest dye to extract and produce, so only royals could afford it. In fact, it would take 12,000 snails to produce 1.4 grams of purple dye.

278. Ants cannot be injured from impact with the ground after being dropped from any height, mostly because they just don't have enough mass.

279. The Concorde jet, that had its last flight in 2003, had a maximum speed of 1,350 miles (2170 km) per hour. It could fly from London, England to New York City in about three hours, about half the time of other passenger planes.

280. On the set of the movie, 'Apocalypse Now', the production cast design decided to actually use real bodies instead of fake ones. It was only discovered when a pungent odor became too strong for the rest of the cast to ignore.

281. There's an annual conference called "The Boring Conference" on boring things. In the past, people have given talks on barcodes, sneezing, and the sounds of vending machines.

282. Astoundingly the human brain, the universe, and the internet all have similar network patterns and the same growth dynamics.

283. Norway offers amazing incentives for people who own electric cars such as, free parking, free charging, and the use of bus lanes. Now so many people in Norway have bought electric cars that the incentives actually have to be rolled back.

284. Sylvan Goldman the inventor of shopping carts, had to hire models to push the carts around in his store to make them more appealing to customers when they first launched.

285. The first-ever 3d feature film was called the Power of Love and premiered in 1922 in Los Angeles. Unfortunately, the 3d version of the film is presumed lost and the 2d version was later shown under the name Forbidden Lover.

286. Christopher Robin Milne, the son of Winnie the Pooh author, A.A Milne, and the person who the character Christopher Robin was based off of, actually hated the books his father wrote and thought it was his father's way of exploiting childhood.

287. The stethoscope was invented in France in 1816 by Rene Laennec because he felt uncomfortable placing his ear on a woman's bare chest in order to listen to her heart.

288. Owen, a baby hippo from Kenya, was swept away from his mother during a tsunami. He then mistook a 130-year-old tortoise for another hippo and the two actually became best friends.

289. The graffiti artist David Choe, who painted Facebook's first office in 2005, was paid in shares and is now worth over $200,000,000.

290. The Sword-billed hummingbird is the only bird with a bill longer than its body.

291. High school student Hayden Godfrey started working several jobs, saved his money for a year and a half, and eventually bought a flower for each of the 834 girls at this school, simply because he wanted them to feel joy.

292. Watching your favorite movie over and over is good for you. The repetition calms you because knowing the outcome of a story helps you to feel safe in an unpredictable world. It also helps comfort you by recapturing lost feelings, according to a study in 2012 by Cristel Antonia Russell and Sidney J. Levy.

293. Ironically 'Finding Nemo', a movie about the anguish of a captured clown fish, caused home aquarium demand to triple. Then that demand was met by large-scale harvesting of tropical fish from the wild, which devastated clown fish populations.

294. In a real world transaction involving Bitcoin a man named Laslow, a computer programmer paid 10,000 Bitcoin for two large Papa John's pizzas. Only four years later those same Bitcoin were worth 5.12 million dollars.

295. Even Al Qaeda has gone on record as denouncing the actions of ISIS as anti-Islamic.

296. A guy named Seth Putnam wrote a song about how being in a coma was stupid, and soon after went into a coma himself. After he awoke, when asked how it felt to be in a coma, he said, "Being in a coma was just as stupid as I wrote it was."

297. Leonardo da Vinci's The Mona Lisa wasn't famous until it was stolen from the Louvre in 1911.

298. A hyena's laugh, which is called giggles by zoologists, can be heard up to 42 feet (13 kilometers) away.

299. Human bone is ridiculously strong. A cubic inch of it can bear the weight of five standard pickup trucks making it four times as strong as concrete.

300. Barbie's full name is Barbara Millicent Roberts. Her creator, Ruth Handler, invented her back in 1959 and named her after her daughter, Barbara. Ken also has a full name too which is Ken Carson.

301. There are giant pink slugs found only in the sub-Alpine reaches of Mount Kaputar, Australia. They can reach up to eight inches long and on a good day, you can see hundreds of them.

302. On D-Day, at least 500 canvased dummies were dropped away from the Normandy Beaches to distract from actual drop zones. The dummies, called ruperts were just under three feet tall, came with battle sounds and were made to self destruct upon landing so that the Germans couldn't find them.

303. Prostitution exists among some penguins and chimpanzees. It was first reported in 1998 by Fiona Hunter, a researcher at the University of Cambridge, and Lloyd Davis of the University of Otago. They were studying the mating patterns of Adelie Penguins when they noticed that they prostitute themselves for things like stones or food.

304. Xiao Yun, from China, was missing for 10 years, and was presumed dead, but was then found living in an internet cafe. A runaway at the age of 14, she was good at the game Crossfire, so other gamers paid to watch her play it and she slept at internet

cafes for the rest of her life and public bathhouses until she was found at the age of 24.

305. When Don Karkos fought in World War II, he was hit with shrapnel that blinded his right eye. 64 years later, while working in a barn, a horse head-butted him in the exact same spot, threw him against a wall and restored his vision suddenly.

306. The FBI now tracks animal abuse like it tracks homicides and assaults. Their logic is that they classify animal cruelty as a group A felony because if you abuse animals, there's a good chance that you'd do the same to a person.

307. According to a study of surgical residents participating in the Rosser Top Gun Laparoscopic Skills and Suturing Program, surgeons who play video games make 37% fewer errors and complete 27% faster. Video game skills are a strong indicator of surgical skills.

308. The CIA once created a gun that could shoot darts that caused heart attacks. Upon penetration of the skin, the dart only left a tiny red dot. The poison itself worked rapidly and then denatured quickly afterward. This was all revealed in 1975, in a congressional testimony.

309. Wu Hsia, from China, had an ex-girlfriend and current girlfriend jump off a bridge into a river to see who he would rescue. He rescued his current girlfriend.

310. Oysters make pearls so that they can feel better. When a grain of sand or debris gets stuck in their bodies, they ease the pain and irritation by coating it with multiple layers of nacre. It's a mineral that lines the inside of their shells, and thus, a pearl begins to form.

311. In the 19th century, Americans purposefully filled their parks with squirrels for entertainment purposes. Before that, they were rarely found outside of forests.

312. Hippopotamus milk is pink.

313. Caesar salad has nothing to do with any of the Caesars. It was first concocted in a bar in Tijuana, Mexico, in the 1920's.

314. Your fingernails grow faster when you are cold.

315. Snails take the longest naps, some lasting as long as three years.
316. Crocodiles and alligators are surprisingly fast on land. Although they are rapid, they are not agile. So, if being chased by one, run in a zigzag line to lose him or her.
317. Octopuses have three hearts.
318. Since 1978, 37 people have died by Vending Machine's falling on them. 13 people are killed annually. All this while trying to shake merchandise out of them. 113 people have been injured.
319. Wild dolphins call each other by name.
320. A grenade blast underwater is more deadly than on land.
321. To escape the grip of a crocodile's jaws, push your thumbs into its eyeballs - it will let you go instantly.
322. Mel Blanc (the voice of Bugs Bunny) was allergic to carrots.
323. Because of the rotation of the earth, an object can be thrown farther if it is thrown west.
324. Half the foods eaten throughout the world today were developed by farmers in the Andes Mountains (including potatoes, maize, sweet potatoes, squash, all varieties of beans, peanuts, manioc, papayas, strawberries, mulberries, and many others).
325. Right-handed people live, on average; nine years longer than left-handed people.
326. If one spells out numbers, they would have to count to One Thousand before coming across the letter "A".
327. Ten percent of the Russian government's income comes from the sale of vodka.
328. The expression 'to get fired' comes from long ago Clans that wanted to get rid of unwanted people, so they would burn their houses instead of killing them, creating the term 'Got fired'.
329. It has been estimated that humans use only 10% of their brain.
330. In the United States, a pound of potato chips costs two hundred times more than a pound of potatoes.
331. If you go blind in one eye you only lose about one-fifth of your vision but all your sense of depth.

332. Celery has negative calories! It takes more calories to eat a piece of celery than the celery has in it.

333. Studies have shown that children laugh an average of 300 times/day and adults 17 times/day, making the average child more optimistic, curious, and creative than the adult.

334. The average woman consumes 6 lbs of lipstick in her lifetime.

335. The phrase "rule of thumb" is derived from an old English law, which stated that you couldn't beat your wife with anything wider than your thumb.

336. Each king in a deck of playing cards represents a great king from history. Spades - King David, Clubs - Alexander the Great, Hearts - Charlemagne, and Diamonds - Julius Caesar.

337. Jupiter is bigger than all the other planets in our solar system combined.

338. Emus and kangaroos cannot walk backward and are on the Australian coat of arms for that reason.

339. There are 1 million ants for every human in the world.

340. The three most recognized Western names in China are Jesus Christ, Richard Nixon, & Elvis Presley.

341. The Pentagon in Arlington, Virginia, has twice as many bathrooms as is necessary because when it was built in the 1940s, the state of Virginia still had segregation laws requiring separate toilet facilities for blacks and whites.

342. Conception occurs most in the month of December.

343. One-third of all cancers are sun related.

344. The average lead pencil will draw a line 35 miles long or write approximately 50,000 English words. More than 2 billion pencils are manufactured each year in the United States. If these were laid end to end they would circle the world nine times.

345. Nearly 80% of all animals on earth have six legs.

346. Larry Lewis ran the 100-yard dash in 17.8 seconds in 1969, thereby setting a new world's record for runners in the 100-years-or-older class. He was 101.

347. Ninety percent of all species that have become extinct have been birds.

348. The only nation whose name begins with an "A", but doesn't end in an "A" is Afghanistan.

349. The Earth experiences 50,000 Earthquakes per year and is hit by Lightning 100 times a second.

350. Hershey's Kisses are called that because the machine that makes them looks like it's kissing the conveyor belt.

351. Statues in parks: If the horse has both front legs in the air, the person died in battle; if the horse has one front leg in the air, the person died as a result of wounds received in battle; if the horse has all four legs on the ground, the person died of natural causes.

352. It has NEVER rained in Calama, a town in the Atacama Desert of Chile.

353. The Main Library at Indiana University sinks over an inch every year because when it was built, engineers failed to take into account the weight of all the books that would occupy the building.

354. 400-quarter pounders can be made from 1 cow.

355. If we had the same mortality rate now as in 1900, more than half the people in the world today would not be alive.

356.   The plastic things on the end of shoelaces are called aglets.

357. Ants closely resemble human manners: When they wake, they stretch & appear to yawn in a human manner before taking up the tasks of the day.

358. A raisin dropped into a glass of fresh champagne will bounce up and down continuously from the bottom of the glass to the top.

359. More Monopoly money is printed in a year, than real money throughout the world.

360. The longest one-syllable word in the English language is "screeched." "Dreamt" is the only English word that ends in the letters "mt."

361. All of the clocks in the movie "Pulp Fiction" are stuck on 4:20, a national pot-smokers hour.

362. A dragonfly has a lifespan of 24 hours.

363. The microwave was invented after a researcher walked by a radar tube and a chocolate bar melted in his pocket.
364. All polar bears are left-handed.
365. If you yelled for 8 years, 7 months and 6 days, you will have produced enough sound energy to heat one cup of coffee.
366. February 1865 is the only month in recorded history not to have a full moon.
367. The top 3 health-related searches on the Internet are (in this order): Depression, Allergies, & Cancer.
368. Dentists have recommended that a toothbrush be kept at least 6 feet away from a toilet to avoid airborne particles resulting from the flush.
369. A family of 26 could go to the movies in Mexico City for the price of one in Tokyo.
370. The muzzle of a lion is like a fingerprint - no two lions have the same pattern of whiskers.
371. The average person spends 12 weeks a year 'looking for things'.
372. The number "four" is considered unlucky in Japan because it is pronounced the same as "death".
373. Venus is the only planet that rotates clockwise.
374. One in eight million people has progeria, a disease that causes people to grow faster than they age.
375. It's estimated that at any one time around 0.7% of the world's population is drunk.
376. During his entire life, Vincent Van Gogh sold exactly one painting, "Red Vineyard at Arles".
377. The word "set" has more definitions than any other word in the English language.
378. In 10 minutes, a hurricane releases more energy than all of the world's nuclear weapons combined.
379. Switzerland is the only country with a square flag.
380. Chocolate can kill dogs; it directly affects their heart and nervous system.
381. There are more beetles than any other animal. In fact, one out of every four animals is a beetle.

382. If you keep a goldfish in the darkroom, it will eventually turn white.

383. In bowling, three strikes in a row was called a turkey. The term originated in the 1800s when at holiday time, the first member of a team to score three strikes in a row won a free turkey.

384. Giraffes have no vocal cords.

385. The idea of Pokémon evolving is actually based on the caterpillar becoming a butterfly. Pokémon creator Satoshi Tajiri loved collecting and studying the creatures as a child and based his worldwide hit on the process.

386. Banana trees are not actually trees – they are giant herbs.

387. To 'hang ten' in surfing, means to have all 10 toes over the edge of the board when riding a wave.

388. The term Quarantine is one that is as old as time, segregating the ill or dangerous to protect the rest of the tribe but where does the phrase come from? The Italian phrase quaranta giorni is said to be the origin of the word quarantine, it means simply 40 days and refers to a time when during the plague ships arriving in Venice were required to stay out at sea for the entire 40 days before docking.

389. 1,800 cigarettes are smoked per person each year in China.

390. Have you ever yawned and a bit of saliva shoots out of your mouth into the air? So have many apparently, you're not alone. This process is known as Gleeking and is caused by your salivary glands being randomly stimulated.

391. In 2015 the Korean Herald revealed a study that found out that the number of fried chicken outlets in Korea stood a whopping 36,000. This figure means the country has almost the same number of these outlets as there are McDonald's branches across the world.

392. The only country in the world to begin with a Q is Qatar, the nearest English pronunciation to the local way would be Cutter and the name comes from Qatara referring to Zubara, a town in the country. The only country ending in Q is Iraq.

393. Fort Knox has an escape tunnel installed in the lower part of the vault. This tunnel is there in case anyone accidentally becomes trapped inside the vault.

394. In ancient Rome, gladiators were held in the highest respect, but one of the rarer sights were female gladiators or gladiatrix, a much less common fighter who had the same purpose as their male counterparts but have all but disappeared from history.

395. A 16-year-old may legally vote in Serbia but only if they are employed citizens. The voting age for those not employed stands at 18, a similar figure to most of the world.

396. In 2015, it was discovered that the number 1 cause of death for policemen is suicide, mainly due to the stress caused by the job itself.

397. A 120-pound woman annihilated a 72-ounce steak challenge in Portland, U.S.A. after clearing the plate in a staggering 2 minutes 44 seconds, a whole 4 minutes faster than the previous holder. That's an average of almost 0.5 ounce per second. The creator of The Sims; Will Wright, created the game after experiencing a tragic house fire in 1991 left him with a vision of a game surrounding a "virtual dollhouse" and the franchise was born.

398. Bananas are curved because they grow towards the sun.

399. The internet speed at NASA is capable of downloading the average film in milliseconds, as its speed is a staggering 91 GB a second.

400. A single snowflake is known as one of the most delicate and miniscule items in the world. However, the largest measured snowflake was a whopping 15 inches wide.

401. Pteronophobia is the fear of being tickled by feathers.

402. In Elizabethan England, the spoon was so novel and prized that people carried their own folding spoons to banquets.

403. 71% of office workers stopped on the street for a survey agreed to give up their computer passwords in exchange for a chocolate bar.

404. So far, two diseases have successfully been eradicated: smallpox and rinderpest.

405. The Olympic flag's colors are always red, black, blue, green, and yellow rings on a field of white. This is because at least one of those colors appears on the flag of every nation on the planet.

406. There are only three types of snakes on the island of Tasmania and all three are deadly poisonous.

407. All major league baseball umpires must wear black underwear while on the job in case their pants split.

408. Ninety percent of New York City cabbies are recently arrived immigrants.

409. In the 16th and 17th centuries in the country of Turkey, anyone caught drinking coffee was put to death.

410. The city with the most Rolls Royces per capita is Hong Kong.

411. In 18th century England, gambling dens employed someone whose job was to swallow the dice if there was a police raid.

412. A Boeing 767 airliner is made of 3,100,000 separate parts.

413. There is a bar in London that sells vaporized vodka, which is inhaled instead of sipped.

414. The longest bout of hiccups lasted nearly 69 years.

415. The largest ocean liners pay a $250,000 toll for each trip through the Panama Canal. The canal generates fully one-third of Panama's entire economy.

416. According to Genesis 1:20-22, the chicken came before the egg.

417. The moon is moving away from the Earth at a tiny, although measurable, rate every year. 85 million years ago it was orbiting the Earth about 35 feet from the planet's surface.

418. Sonic the Hedgehog's full name is actually Ogilvie Maurice Hedgehog.

419. In Egypt around 1500 B.C., a shaved head was considered the ultimate in feminine beauty. Egyptian women removed every hair from their heads with special gold tweezers and polished their scalps to a high sheen with buffing cloths.

420. The stage before frostbite is called "frostnip".

421. There is enough fuel in full jumbo jet tank to drive an average car four times around the world.

422. A kiss stimulates 29 muscles and chemicals that cause relaxation.
423. There is a company that will (for $14,000) take your ashes and compress them into a synthetic diamond to be set in jewelry for a loved one.
424. Your heart beats over 100,000 times a day.
425. Snakes are true carnivores as they eat nothing but other animals. They do not eat any type of plant material.
426. The chicken is one of the few things that man eats before it's born and after it's dead.
427. A duel between three people is actually called a truel.
428. The Himalayan Honey Bee – the largest of the honey bees – makes a hallucinogenic honey that tribes collect.
429. The brain is our fattiest organ, being composed of nearly 60% fat.
430. The collars on men's dress shirts used to be detachable. This was to save on laundry costs as the collar was the part that needed cleaning the most frequently.
431. Sunsets on Mars are blue.
432. The Vatican City is the country that drinks the most wine per capita at 74 liters per citizen per year.
433. Eight of the ten largest statues in the world are of Buddhas.
434. A small population of Mammoths survived on Wrangel Island until 1650 BC, about 900 years after the construction of The Great Pyramid of Giza were completed.
435. The Flintstones was the most profitable network cartoon franchise for 30 years, that's before The Simpsons came along.
436. Homosexuality was still classified as an illness in Sweden in 1979. Swedes responded by calling into work "sick," saying they "felt gay."
437. If a female ferret does not have sex for a year, she will die.
438. People don't sneeze in their sleep due to their brain shutting down the reflex.
439. If you made $1 every second, it would take you 2,921 years to have more money than Bill Gates (over 92.1 billion dollars).

440. Iguanas have three eyes. Two normal eyes and a third eye on top of their head that only perceives brightness.
441. 'Digging a hole to China' is theoretically possible if you start in Argentina.
442. Some areas in Scotland and Japan switched to blue street lights at night and saw a decrease in crime & suicide rates.
443. The oldest condoms ever found date back to the 1640s (they were found in a cesspit at Dudley Castle), and were made from animal and fish intestines.
444. Female kangaroos have three vaginas.
445. The northern leopard frog swallows its prey using its eyes — it uses them to help push food down its throat by retracting them into its head.
446. Experiments show that male rhesus macaque monkeys will pay to look at pictures of female rhesus macaques' bottoms.
447. There's an opera house on the U.S.–Canada border where the stage is in one country and half the audience is in another.
448. Humans are the Only Animals That Enjoy Spicy Foods.
449. Dogs can smell cancer. Researchers have found that dogs are able to pick up on a specific scent that cancer produces in a person—which is undetectable to humans.
450. The average four-year-old child asks over four hundred questions a day.
451. More than 2,500 left-handed people are killed every year from using equipment meant for right-handed people.
452. Potato Chips Cause More Weight Gain Than Any Other Food.
453. If "The Simpsons" aged normally, Bart would now be older than Marge was in the first season.
454. The population of Ireland is still 2 million less than it was before the potato famine, 160 years ago.
455. The average hummingbird's heart rate is more than 1,200 beats per minute.
456. If the human brain were a computer, it could perform 38 thousand-trillion operations per second. The world's most

powerful supercomputer, BlueGene, can manage only .002% of that.

457. You have a 1 in 200 chance of being related to Genghis Khan.

458. Along with the five traditional senses of sound, sight, touch, smell, and taste, humans have 15 "other senses." These include balance, temperature, pain and time as well as internal senses for suffocation, thirst, and fullness.

459. There is a single mega-colony of ants that spans three continents, covering much of Europe, the west coast of the U.S., and the west coast of Japan.

460. Airplane food isn't very tasty because our sense of smell and taste decrease by 20 to 50 percent during flights.

461. Some of the first examples of graffiti come from 1st century Pompeii, where messages like "I don't want to sell my husband" and "Successus was here" were written on walls.

462. Sloths will mistakenly grab their arms instead of the branches of a tree, which can lead to fatal falls.

463. The world's longest musical piece lasts 639 years.

464. France didn't stop executing people by guillotine until 1977.

465. Craving ice is a symptom of iron deficiency.

466. Though closely identified as a female fashion staple today, high heels were first designed for men.

467. Your sense of touch fades as you age.

468. Tuskless elephants are evolving in response to poaching.

469. Male pufferfish create "crop circles" to attract mates.

470. There's a city in Turkey called Batman, located in the province of Batman near the Batman River.

471. A Shiba Inu dog named 'Body' makes $180,000 a year modeling menswear on Instagram.

472. According to textbooks used to teach children in North Korea, Kim Jong-un learned to drive at the age of three.

473. There are so many different types of apples, if you were to eat a new one every day it would take you almost 20 years to try them all.

474. In India, it's not uncommon to enjoy marijuana in milkshake form. In fact, there's evidence of its consumption in this manner dating all the way back to sometime between 500 and 1500 BC.

475. The CEO of Netflix, Reed Hastings, offered a form of partnership to Blockbuster in the late '90s, and the CEO of Blockbuster, John Antioco, laughed in his face.

476. The Toyota Supra, which Paul Walker's character Brian drives off at the end of Furious 7, actually belonged to the late actor.

477. Apple got the idea of a desktop interface from Xerox.

478. Scientists have found a way to unboil egg whites in a matter of minutes. The major ingredient to pull off this reversal was urea, one of the main components in urine.

479. Dr. Seuss was confronted by a feminist named Alison Lurie, who stated that there are no strong female roles in his books. Near the end of his life, Dr. Seuss replied, stating that his characters are animals, and, "If she can identify their sex "I will remember her in my will."

480. Central American stingless bees have been cultivated by Mayans for thousands of years, and have been regarded as pets with their hives hung in and around the home. Some hives have been recorded to last over 80 years, being passed down through the generations.

481. Recent polling indicated that 35% of U.S. workers would willingly forego a substantial raise in exchange for seeing their direct supervisor fired.

482. Jonathan the tortoise is a giant tortoise who lives on the island of St. Helena in the South Pacific Ocean that's believed to have been born in 1832 and is still alive to this day.

483. If you multiply 111,111,111 by 111,111,111, it gives the magical, mathematical result of 12,345,678,987,654,321.

484. The original release date of Halo 2 for the PC was delayed because Microsoft discovered that one of the developers hid a picture of his ass in it.

485. The lowest class of meat is called canner and comes from very old cows with little fat in their tough meat and is used in both dog food and school lunches

486. In 2013 Volkswagen succeeded in building a car that gets 235 miles per gallon called the XL1. Almost the entire car is made out of carbon fiber and only weighs 81 kilograms.

487. Most of the time, the ice-cream that you see in TV commercials and other ads, is actually mashed potatoes. This is because regular ice-cream wouldn't be able to stand up to the heat of the onset lights while filming.

488. If you are an Indian American, and you own a motel, there is a 70% chance that your last name is Patel.

489. The reason men have nipples is because all embryos start off as females in the womb.

490. According to researchers night owls, or people who stay up late and sleep in, tend to be more extravagant, impulsive, and novelty seeking. They also tend to be more likely to develop addictive behaviors, mental disorders, and antisocial tendencies.

491. In Stockholm Sweden, there was a temporary campaign implemented called the Speed Camera Lottery where good drivers could win money from the fines of other speeding drivers.

492. The Salar De Uyuni in Bolivia is the world's largest salt flat at ten thousand five hundred and eighty-two square kilometers and turns into the world's largest mirror when it rains. It's so beautiful that it's been called the border between heaven and earth.

493. In Japan, Nestle has introduced over 200 different flavors of Kitkat since 2000, including ginger ale, soy sauce, crème brulee, green tea, and banana.

494. Bob Marley was seen as a white man in his native Jamaica due to having a British father, and he suffered racism and discrimination while growing up.

495. As of 2016 Madeline Scotto was a 101-year-old woman that is still teaching math at the same elementary school in Brooklyn that she graduated from back in 1928.

496. The country of Liechtenstein has an incarceration rate of 19 per 100,000. With a population of only 37,000, this means that there are approximately seven people in prison within the nation.

497. 20-year-old Julien Barreaux from France spent six months looking for the person who killed his online character in a virtual knife fight during a game of Counter Strike. He finally found the culprit living only a few miles away, and then stabbed him in the chest.

498. Flipping a coin isn't actually 50/50, but rather 51/49 biased for the side that was facing up when flipped.

499. The Russians partied so hard once that the entire city of Moscow ran out of vodka.

500. Bob Ross did the 'Joy of Painting' completely free of charge and only made money through his art supply store.

501. In 2015 a goat was placed in a Siberian Tiger enclosure in the Far Eastern Safari Park in Russia, and it was supposed to become the tiger's food, except that the tiger and the goat became friends.

502. According to research done in 2014, people who are perfectionists are at an increased risk of experiencing suicidal thoughts because of the strong social pressure that they feel.

503. Cerro Rico in Bolivia is known as the mountain that eats men, because of the large number of men who have died there while working in the mines. In fact, historians have estimated that about 8 million men have died in the mines since the sixteenth century.

504. The Muppet Show received a letter from a man informing them that the Swedish chef doesn't actually speak Swedish. The head writer wrote back, "Thank you for bringing this to our attention. We were going to fire the chef on the spot but he has a wife and family and promised to take "Swedish lessons."

505. The day after Robin Williams' suicide, the National Suicide Prevention Lifeline fielded the greatest number of calls in its history.

506. The Lego movie incorporated actual fan-made short Lego films into its plot. You can see them on the monitors in the scene where the citizens discover their creativity.

507. Platypuses don't have stomachs.

508. The police in West Germany located a man who had a warrant for unpaid fines. They confronted him just as a slot machine that he was at struck a jackpot and he avoided jail time by paying the fine on the spot.

509. A school in Pune, India encourages students to conserve water by pouring leftover drinking water from the bottles in a large tank before they go home every day. They use this to water for plants and trees or for other non-drinking purposes.

510. Tasmania has an extra day of Easter, known as Easter Tuesday. It is not celebrated anywhere else on Earth.

511. In 2013, Google established a company called Calico that focuses on health, well-being, and longevity. However, what's weird about it isn't that its goal is to extend human life but that it's to cure death.

512. Scotland has the most concentrated pattern of private ownership in the entire world. Only 432 people owned half of the private land there.

513. After visiting Cambodia in 2002, Angelina Jolie bought a sprawling area of land in the northern province of Battambang which was infamous for being poached and turned it into a nature reserve. She was awarded citizenship in response to her actions in 2005.

514. Viganella, Italy is cut off from direct sunlight for 83 days in the winter due to the surrounding mountains so they set up a giant, computer-controlled mirror on the top of the mountainside to reflect the sun's rays onto the town.

515. Slovakia and Slovenia are so often confused that the staff of Slovak and Slovenian embassies have to meet once a month to exchange wrongly addressed mail.

516. The mortar used in the construction of the great pyramids of Giza is of unknown origin. It's been analyzed and while the chemical

composition is known, it cannot be reproduced and is stronger than stone. This is why it's still holding up today and was built sometime between 2540 and 2560 BC.

517. According to a study done in 2013 by Doctor Peter Jonassen from the University of Western Sydney School of Sciences and Psychology, people who wake up late at night are more likely to display antisocial personality traits, such as machiavellianism, narcissism and have psychopathic tendencies.

518. The extinct Dodo bird got its name from the Dutch. They called the bird Dodoor Ursine which loosely translates to fat-asses.

519. One of the top vasectomy doctors in Austin is named Dick Chop.

520. Drug lord Pablo Escobar offered to pay off Columbia's $20 billion foreign debt in order to avoid extradition to the United States.

521. When given the choice between normal water and morphine water, secluded rats always choose the drugged water, and would always die. However, rats provided with space, friends, and games rarely took the drug water and never became addicted or overdosed despite many attempts made by humans to trick them.

522. During the 18th century, you could pay your admission to the zoo in the Tower of London by bringing a cat or a dog to feed the lions.

523. Members of the band Good Charlotte used to heavily protest against KFC's treatment of chickens. Then in 2012 and 2013 they appeared in a number of KFC commercials in Australia, and even tried to set a new world record for eating KFC on Australia's Got Talent.

524. Abraham Lincoln once said, "Women are the only things that cannot hurt me that I am afraid of."

525. Africanized bees, known as "killer bees" are bred hybrids that accidentally escaped quarantine and since have spread throughout the Americas.

526. A stray junkyard dog named Lillico walked up to 13 kilometers every night through the streets of San Carlos, Brazil, to collect a

food parcel. Upon returning home she shares the food with her family, a dog, a cat, some chickens, and a mule.

527. Your body paralyzes itself when you sleep to keep you from acting out your dreams. However, it is in fact possible to wake up still paralyzed, known as "sleep paralysis".

528. In 2013 a cat named Cookie went missing while on holiday with her owner in Grasse, Southern France. Eighteen months later, Cookie returned dirty and emaciated, having traveled a journey of 1127 kilometers all the way home.

529. At the age of only five Ayan Qureshi took and passed Microsoft's IT technician exam, making him the youngest computer specialist in the world.

530. If you earn more than $27,665 Canadian a year, you are part of the richest 4% of the planet.

531. A tomato plant was found on an isolated 40-year-old volcanic island known as Surtsey, found off the coast of Iceland. It was from a previous scientist who took a dump and subsequently a plant grew from there.

532. There's a restaurant called "Tacsiyapo Isdaan Floating Restaurant" in Tarlac City, Philippines, where you are actually allowed to smash plates on the wall to help release pent-up anger.

533. If we were able to capture just 0.1% of the ocean's kinetic energy caused by its tides, we would be able to satisfy the current global demand for energy five times over.

534. Sniper bullets travel so fast that the rotation of the Earth will actually move the target, so shooters have to adjust their aim accordingly.

535. The tires for the Bugatti Veyron cost $42,000 a set and they only last 15 minutes at top speed.

536. According to some experts, it costs only $14 to produce a pair of Beats by Dre headphones. That's a huge profit for Dr. Dre considering the cheapest pair sells for $200 while the most expensive pair retails for 700.

537. A study in 2013 shows that bottlenose dolphins have the longest memories in the animal kingdom. In fact, they can remember the whistles of other dolphins that they've lived with even after 20 years of separation.

538. A man named Paz crashed Paris Hilton's 30th birthday party and stole her $3,200 birthday cake when he realized that no one there was actually going to eat it. He ended up splitting the cake into 125 pieces and served it all to the homeless.

539. The metallic smell of money is actually your body oils breaking down in the presence of iron or copper. You can see this by using a paper towel to pick up a penny and smelling it, no odor.

540. Sarcasm is believed to boost creativity in all parties involved in the conversation.

541. When cats look at you in the eye and blink slowly, they're actually trying to tell you that they're in love with you.

542. The 'Rekonect Notebook' is a magnetic journal that allows you to remove, reattach, and rearrange the pages whenever you want.

543. There is an island called Hans Island, which is disputed territory between Canada and Denmark. The militaries of both countries periodically visit to remove the other guy's flag and leave a bottle of Danish schnapps or Canadian whiskey.

544. Adele isn't allowed to send out her own tweets because when Twitter first came out, she was notorious for tweeting while drunk.

545. Inspired by the viral photo of Donald Trump sporting a man bun, DesignCrowd held a Photoshop contest to see what past and present politicians would look like if they had one.

546. Have you ever noticed that old books have a distinct smell? That's because organic compounds in paper break down over time and release chemicals that smell like vanilla, almonds, and grass.

547. The pangolin is a mammal that looks like a reptile because of its scales. Its scales are made of keratin, which is the same material as human fingernails.

548. Hans Zimmer, the music composer for over 150 movies has never had any formal music education.

549. A teenager in Taiwan died after playing the video game Diablo 3 for 40 hours straight without eating.

550. The phrase happy wife, happy life is actually pretty accurate. A study conducted in 2014 shows that men who are unhappily married may still be happy with their lives in general if their wives are satisfied with their marriages.

551. Former Venezuelan President Hugo Chavez stated that Muammar Gaddafi was welcomed in Venezuela, but stated that Charlie Sheen was not. With a quote saying: "there are limits..."

552. There's a Detroit company called 'Extreme Kidnapping' where people pay up to $1500 to get tied up and kidnapped for fun.

553. Back in 1993, it was discovered that Heidelberg University in Germany was using human corpses in crash tests.

554. Hydrogen peroxide is not recommended for cuts and wounds and actually slows healing by killing the healthy skin cells.

555. In 2010, after the BP oil spill, Stephen Colbert declared that every time he said the word "Bing", the Microsoft search engine would donate $2500 to oil spill cleanup efforts. He managed to say "bing" 40 times, thereby raising $100,000 for his charity, the Colbert Nation Gulf of America fund.

556. Singles Day in China is the world's biggest online shopping day since unattached individuals celebrate by buying themselves gifts.

557. When Paris fell to the Nazis in 1940, French soldiers cut the elevator cables to the Eiffel Tower. They did this so that if Hitler wanted to hoist a swastika flag, they would have to climb hundreds of stairs to get to the top.

558. The original floats in the Macy's Thanksgiving Parade were released into the air, after the parade, because Macy's didn't know what to do with them. However, they included a ticket that would fall to the ground after they popped. If you found a ticket, you could redeem them for a prize at Macy's.

559. California uses inmates to fight forest fires, and prisoners gladly take the jobs, because it reduces their sentence, gets them outside, and pays better than the typical job.

560. The whiptail lizard is an all-female species. The males have gone completely extinct. Interestingly, they are not hermaphroditic. The females actually lay and hatch from unfertilized eggs.

561. The Harry Potter series has been translated into more than 70 languages.

562. President Barack Obama has won two Grammy Awards before he was elected. They were for best-spoken word album, one for an audio recording of his 1995 memoir Dreams from My Father, and the second was for The Audacity of Hope.

563. The Golden Gate Bridge uses the largest bridge cables ever made. They were so long that they could actually encircle the world more than three times at the equator.

564. The world's largest coin was issued by the Royal Canadian Mint back in 2007. It was 20 inches in diameter and one inch thick. It was made of 99.999% gold bullion, weighs 220 pounds and is worth an estimated $1 million.

565. In 1967, St. Paul, Alberta, Canada, built the world's first UFO landing pad. The 130-ton structure consists of a raised platform with a map of Canada embossed on the backstop consisting of stones provided by each province in Canada. The pad also has a time capsule to be opened on the 100 year anniversary of the pad's opening in 2067.

566. There are wildlife overpasses, green bridges and ecoducts that exist that were built over roads to allow wildlife to cross safely to the other side. They are up to 197 feet wide. The larger ones are to accommodate large mammals such as bears, wolves and moose and deer. They're covered in soil and vegetation to provide a suitable habitat for a wide range of groups of animals.

567. In Japan, if you're in someone's home and you need to use the bathroom, you need to change out of your house slippers and into toilet slippers. Not only that but then you need to remove the toilet slippers before exiting the washroom.

568. There's a nightclub in Devon, U.K., who gave out free lollipops to reduce late-night rowdiness in hopes that drunken clubbers

wouldn't be able to shout or cause disturbance while sucking on them, and it worked.

569. Einstein actually had an illegitimate daughter that was born in 1902.

570. In the 1990s, Saddam Hussein had the Quran transcribed by an Islamic calligrapher in his own blood. He had over seven gallons of blood drawn over a two-year period.

571. The voice of Chewbacca from Star Wars was created by using bear vocalizations, as well as the sound of walruses, badgers, and the howls of sick animals.

572. The opossum is the only marsupial in North America.

573. Walmart employs 2.3 million people around the world.

574. Boston has poems on their sidewalks that can only be seen when it rains. They are painted with special waterproof paint that only appears when wet.

575. At the 2008 Olympics in Beijing, white mice were fed 24 hours before the athletes were fed to protect the athletes from food poisoning. If there was a problem, the food could be traced and destroyed before being fed to the athletes.

576. A 19-foot-long (1.5 meter) Australian alligator has a bite force of 3,700 pounds (1700 kg). That's the highest bite force ever recorded.

577. On January 12th, 2011, 49 out of the 50 states of America had snow on the ground. That's almost 71% of the country. The only state without snow was Florida.

578. Theodore Roosevelt's mother and first wife both died on Valentine's Day of 1884. His mother died of typhoid fever, and 12 hours later his wife died from Bright's disease and complications from giving birth to the couple's first child two days before.

579. Actor Steven Seagull received a PETA humanitarian award in 1999 for preventing the export of baby elephants from South Africa to Japan.

580. The Island of Discussion in Scotland is where, historically, those with arguments were put on the island with cheese and whiskey

to sort out their problems and couldn't leave until they came to a mutual agreement.

581. Breakups are actually more painful for men. In a study of around 5,705 participants from 96 countries, it was found that while women experience intense pain immediately after a breakup, they get over it pretty quickly, men on the other hand, move on quickly but remain damaged for longer.

582. There is a limestone wall in Bolivia that is home to over 5,000 dinosaur footprints, some of them dating back nearly 68 million years.

583. Crows have actually been shown to be as smart as great apes. They are able to show imagination, anticipation of possible future events, and are able to solve problems which require abstract reasoning.

584. There is a Chinese Segway rip-off company called NineBot, which used the money that it got from selling rip-off Segways to buy the original Segway Company.

585. There exists a giant American wasp with a sting so painful one peer-reviewed journal advises anyone who gets stung to lie down and scream to avoid further injury.

586. In the 1970s, people in Cambodia were killed for being academics or for merely wearing sunglasses.

587. April 11th, 1954 is known as the most boring day in history. Literally not a single memorable thing happened that day on the entire earth. No one significant died, no major events occurred, and the only interesting thing that actually happened on that day is that nothing happened on that day.

588. In the Meiji era in japan there was a custom called Autoguru where people dyed their teeth black. It prevented tooth decay and during the time was actually seen as beautiful.

589. Napoleon Bonaparte wore his black, felted, beaver fur hat sideways instead of with the points at the front and back so that he could be easily spotted on the battlefield.

590. In China, there's a delicacy called Virgin Boy Eggs. These eggs are actually soaked in the urine of boys under the age of 10 and

they collect the urine from school washrooms. It's believed that eating this can have health benefits. You can buy one for about 24 cents.

591. In South Korea, you could have a plastic surgery called smile lipped, where they raise both corners of your mouth and give you a permanent smile.

592. In China, you can buy baby Buddha shaped pears. The farmers clamp a mold onto a growing fruit to get the shape. In addition to baby pears, a company called Fruit Mold manufacturers heart-shaped cucumbers, square watermelons and other more deliciously odd shapes.

593. At the Austrian Brewer's Starkenberger's castle, you can actually swim in beer. They have seven 13-foot pools filled with 42,000 pints of warm beer and some water where you can sit and relax completely immersed. The beer's rich in vitamins and calcium and it's thought that sitting in it is good for the skin and can help cure open wounds and psoriasis.

594. It can actually be considered rude to tip in Japan. If you do decide to tip something, the proper etiquette is to place the money in a tasteful, decorative envelope, seal it, and then hand it to the recipient with a slight bow.

595. The Philippines is the only country in the world that denies divorce to the majority of its citizens. They can file for legal separation, which will allow them to separate their possessions and live apart, but does not legally end the marital union and thus, does not permit remarriage.

596. German sneaker company Nat-2 has created the first vegan wooden sneaker. They're made of up to 90% real sustainable wood, which is applied to an organic cotton and vector engraved in a way that the material bends and becomes soft and flexible like fine leather.

597. Tigers are nicer than lions. Lions fight to the death over a kill, but tigers that come across other tigers while hunting often share their meals. Male tigers even wait for females and their cubs to eat first.

598. According to psychologist Adrian Furnham, perfectionism can be a curse that often leads to depression. The reason for this is because perfectionists often have an unrealistic view about failure and are overly critical of themselves, which results in having a very negative impact on their daily lives.

599. Research conducted at the University of Warsaw concluded that the average person is able to accurately track three to four moving objects at any one time. However, an avid action gamer can track six to seven.

600. Scientology isn't legally considered a religion at all in many countries. In fact, Switzerland identifies it as a commercial enterprise, France and Chile as a cult, and Norway as a nonprofit.

601. During the Iranian embassy siege in London, England back in 1980, when given the choice of who from the group of hostages would be released, they chose Ali Guil Ghanzafar, whose loud snoring was keeping them awake.

602. The Megamouth shark, first discovered back in 1976, is a species of shark that is so rare that only 60 of them have ever been captured or identified on record.

603. For eight consecutive years, a Greyhound dog named Jasmine, who survived in a shelter, was the surrogate mother to over 50 rescued animals, including puppies, foxes, four badger cubs, 15 chicks, eight guinea pigs, 15 rabbits, deer, and a goose!

604. In a study conducted by data scientist Matt Daniels, all members of the Wu-Tang Clan are all in the top 20 of artists with the largest vocabulary in the world.

605. Eiffel Tower designer, Gustave Eiffel included a secret apartment for himself near the top, where he would entertain elite members of the science community.

606. Research from the University College of London concluded that teenagers are scientifically less empathetic than adults. Due to the continual development in their brains, teenagers are less likely to use the neural area that is associated with guilt and empathy when they make decisions.

607. Leonidas of Sparta was not a young man at the Battle of Thermopylae, like depicted in the film 300. In reality, he was actually more like 60-years-old.

608. Al Capone was known for sending flowers to rival gang members' funerals. In fact, at one time, he actually spent over $5,000 on a single funeral.

609. The average fast food customer eats about 12 pubic hairs a year.

610. The word "best" in best man historically refers to his skill with a sword. This is because he may have been needed it if the bride tried to run away, or if her family tried to stop the wedding.

611. Jellyfish are 98% water, so when they wash up on the shore, they will eventually simply evaporate into the sun.

612. In 2015, Oscar Santillan, an artist from Ecuador, removed one inch off the peak of England's highest mountain, Scafell Pike. In response, the British demanded that that inch be returned to them, and accused him of vandalism.

613. After an 8.0 magnitude earthquake that hit Mexico City in 1985, a hospital collapsed, yet four newborn babies survived for seven days trapped under the rubble. They have become known as the miracle babies for surviving without nourishment, water, or human contact for so long.

614. The CEO of Japan Airlines, Todu Yamanaka makes less than the pilots, takes a bus to work, and eats in the cafeteria. When interviewed about his, he said that businesses who pursue money first, fail.

615. Chuck Palahniuk, author of the Fight Club, preferred the film adaptation so much that it actually made him embarrassed of his own book.

616. The mathematical proof that one plus one equals two actually takes 162 pages to explain. It was documented in a three-volume work called "Principia Mathematica", which details the foundations of mathematics.

617. In an attempt to get fit and lose weight, 54-year-old Cong Yan from Jilin, China walked daily with an 88-pound rock balanced on his head.

618. Seven Cent Brewery located in Australia has created a beer using the yeast isolated from the belly button lint of it's brewers.

619. London England has a clothing optional restaurant called Bunyadi. It costs up to $95 a person for food and drinks and you can choose between clothed and naked and pure seating areas where you will be served by semi-nude staff.

620. The Dutch apparel company, Cover, has created jackets and bags that feature technology that blocks every in and outgoing signal making the wearer completely untraceable by modern tracking devices, such as computer chips embedded in credit cards and can even take you off the cell phone grid.

621. Product and graphic designer, Ricky Ma, constructed a life-sized robot that looks exactly like Scarlett Johansson. It took him a year and a half and cost him $50,000.

622. Mount Everest actually shrank one inch in 2015, due to the earthquake in Nepal.

623. Ring announcer Michael Buffer has made over 400 million dollars by licensing the use of the trademark catchphrase, "Let's get ready to..."

624. FANUC, a Japanese robotics company, has a factory that can run unsupervised for 30 days at a time. Robots build other robots at a rate of 50 per 24 hour shift. These factories are called lights-out factories, because no human presence is needed.

625. The Van Cats of Eastern Turkey, which are naturally occurring breed, all have white fur, mismatched eyes, and love to swim.

626. In 2009, a man named Alexei Roskov from Russia, drank three bottles of vodka, and then jumped out of a five story window, walked back up, and jumped out again, because of his nagging wife, and he survived.

627. Drew Manning is a personal trainer, who in 2011, wanted to prove that it was possible to get back in shape, even if you become extremely overweight. He gained 32 kilograms, or 70 pounds of fat, over a six month period, before he started the tough journey back to regaining his prior form.

628. You can see underwater sea life and coral reefs using Google Maps.

629. Adnan and Sana Klaric, a married couple from Zenica, Bosnia, started cheating on each other in online chat rooms. When they finally decided to meet up with the person that they were each cheating with, they quickly realized that they had been cheating on each other, and soon after, filed for divorce.

630. The Pronghorn Antelope has 10-times the vision of humans, which has left scientists to believe that on a clear night, they can actually see the rings of Saturn.

631. Russian Special Forces use a knife that fires a bullet out of the bottom of the hilt. The safe way to fire it involves holding the blade to absorb the recoil.

632. A terminally ill six-year-old boy named Levi Mayhew was offered a gift from the Make-A-Wish Foundation. Instead of using it for himself, he wished a trip to Disneyland for the little girl writing him letters out of encouragement, and she went to Florida, carrying a cutout photo of him on all the rides that she could.

633. Serial killer Rodney Alcala acted as his own attorney in his trial in 2010. For five hours, he interrogated himself on the witness stand, asking questions addressed to Mr. Alcala in a deep voice and answering them in his normal voice.

634. There is an entire industry to help students cheat to get their degrees, by having their papers written by unemployed graduates and professors and it's actually kind of brilliant, because students can't get caught for plagiarism, because the papers are brand new.

635. Scorpion venom is the most expensive liquid on Earth, at 39-million dollars per gallon.

636. Usain Bolt ate nothing but chicken nuggets while he was in Beijing for the 2008 Summer Olympics, because he found Chinese food to be odd.

637. When Teddy Roosevelt was a child he had debilitating asthma, except that doctors didn't understand the disease at the time and told him to smoke cigars, drink coffee, and whisky.

638. Domestic animals are a lot smarter than you might realize. In fact, some pets will actually pretend to be sick just to get special attention from their owners.

639. In Finland there's an annual contest called Eukonkanto where men race to carry their wives through an obstacle course. The winner receives his wife's weight in beer.

640. Sloths can swim three times faster than they can move on land and can hold their breath underwater for up to 40 minutes.

641. 1.5 million people were evicted from their homes in Beijing in preparation for the 2008 Olympics.

642. At El Diablo restaurant in the Canary Islands, food is served with the geothermal heat from an actual volcano.

643. A photo of nine-year-old Daniel Cabrera from the Philippines doing his homework in the street, assisted by the light of a local McDonald's resulted in the world donating money, school supplies and a college scholarship to both him and his family.

644. When Benjamin Franklin died in 1790, he willed the cities of Boston and Philadelphia $4,400 each but with the stipulation that the money could not be spent for 200 years. By 1990, Boston's trust was worth over $5 million.

645. In ancient Egypt, men could take time off work to care for menstruating daughters and wives.

646. New Zealand will deny people residency visas if they have too high of a BMI, and there have been cases of people rejected simply because of their weight.

647. Stephen Hawking has said outside of our own universe, lies another, different universe, and in this universe, Zayn is still in One Direction.

648. On July 23, 1983, Air Canada Flight 143 with 69 people on board ran out of fuel at an altitude of 12.5 kilometers. Miraculously, the pilot managed to glide the plane down safely, as he was a very experienced glider pilot. Additionally, 2,300 pounds of jet fuel had been put in instead of 2,300 kilograms.

649. The city of Lexington, Kentucky is letting residents pay parking tickets with canned food donations during the holiday season.

650. Hong Kong billionaire Cecil Chao is offering 120 million dollars to turn his lesbian daughter straight.

651. Don't ever place a cucumber behind your cat. It's stressful for the cat to find a new object in its territory and could leave it anxious for days.

652. Sir Ian McKellen actually broke down and cried while filming the Hobbit, because he had to film with just a green screen instead of with the other actors. In fact, he was quoted as saying, "This is not why I became an actor."

653. In 2015, Daniella Perez, a woman in a wheelchair who had no feet, won a treadmill and a walk-in sauna on the Price is Right.

654. In 1955, cigarettes were sold in vending machines that only accept quarters, but a pack of cigarettes only used to cost 23 cents. Instead of raising the price, cigarette manufacturers actually included two pennies within each package.

655. In the town of Laguna, Brazil, a pod of Bottlenose Dolphins have been cooperatively fishing with fishermen since 1846. The dolphin herd mullet fish towards the shore and signal the fishermen to cast their nets.

656. In 2014, a man spent over $40,000 buying out two IMAX theaters in Beijing because his ex-girlfriend seven years prior had dumped him for not being able to afford movie tickets.

657. During World War I, Allied soldiers would fire thousands of rounds at random over the German trenches to boil the coolant water in their machine guns so that they could make tea.

658. There's a hotel atop the Foronon del Buinz mountain in the Julian Alps that accommodates only nine people. Guests can stay there for free as long as they're willing to make the 8030 feet (2530 meter) hike to get there.

659. In 1965, a 16-year-old high school student Randy Gardner stayed awake for 11 days and 24 minutes. That's 265 hours straight. He holds the record for a human intentionally staying awake without the use of stimulants.

660. To honor Jamaican sprinter Usain Bolt, Berlin gave him his own 12-foot-high (3.66 meters) piece of the Berlin Wall. It weighed nearly three tons.

661. The richest man in Hong Kong, billionaire Li Ka-shing, dropped out of school before he turned 16. He has an estimated net worth of $20.1 billion.

662. LSD or acid was legal in California up until 1966.

663. In 1980, Detroit gave Saddam Hussein the key to the city.

664. The olm salamander has a maximum lifespan of over 100 years.

665. South Africa's Witwatersrand Basin which is only 2.7 square miles (3 square kilometers), has produced more gold than any other continent; about 50,000 tons over 120 years, which is nearly half the gold ever mined.

666. There's a pub in Athlone, Ireland, called Sean's Bar that has been open since 900 AD.

667. The seawater in Boston Harbor in Massachusetts Bay has been found to contain caffeine. Although tiny, the traces are there. 140 to 1,600 nanograms in the Boston Harbor and 5.2 to 71 nanograms in Massachusetts Bay.

668. Samuel J. Seymour was the last surviving witness of Abraham Lincoln's assassination. He lived long enough that he was able to talk about his experience on a TV show in 1956.

669. Potatoes absorb and reflect radio wave signals the same way that human bodies do. So in the past engineers have actually used them to test and improve Wifi signals on planes.

670. An ornithologist named George Archibald managed to save the whooping crane species from becoming extinct, by spending 37 years acting as a mate to a female whooping crane who thought she was human. He finally got her to mate with a real bird and the rest is history.

671. William Shakespeare has added over 2200 words to the English language. Some of those words are, newfangled, bedazzled, and swagger.

672. The Dead Sea has an unusually high salt concentration with about eight to nine times more salt than natural seawater. This

means that people can easily float in the Dead Sea because of its natural buoyancy.

673. There's an artist named Mariusz Kedzierski, who was born without arms, but never gave up on his dreams and has won global awards for his photo realistic portrait drawings.

674. Stress literally kills your brain. Studies have found that months of exposure to stress can permanently destroy neurons in your brain, which affects learning, impulse control, reasoning, and memory.

675. A hungry sea lion pup once walked into a fancy San Diego restaurant, and sat down at a prime table with an ocean view.

676. During World War I, Woodrow Wilson kept a flock of 48 sheep on the White House lawn to save money on groundskeepers. The sheep also earned 52,823 dollars for the Red Cross through the auction of their wool.

677. In 1928, the founder of the Kodak Company was so frustrated by the different numbers of days in each month that he insisted that the company operates on a 13 month year. Each month had exactly four weeks, and they did this all the way up to 1989.

678. 10 squats will get you a free subway ticket in Mexico City. The government offers this to residents in hopes of fighting obesity in the country where 70% of adults are actually overweight.

679. There's a village in Kerala, India called Kodinhi, with just 2,000 families and has around 200 pairs of twins and no one knows why this high occurrence of multiple births happens.

680. According to a survey, 51% of people believe that sharing a Netflix password with a significant other means the relationship is serious.

681. Thanks to 3D printing, it is now possible for blind expectant mothers to have a three-dimensional ultrasound printed for them to sense the image of their unborn child.

682. Banks have therapists known as wealth psychologists who help super-rich clients who are mentally unable to cope with their immense wealth.

683. Blair McMillan from Guelph, Ontario, Canada, was concerned that his family was becoming too attached to technology, so they spent the entirety of the year 2013 living like it was 1986, with a rotary phone, boom box and tube television.

684. Research conducted by NASA in 1995 concluded that the perfect nap lasts for about 26 minutes.

685. Tesla Motors doesn't spend any money on advertising. Instead, they put all of their money into making their cars as good as possible.

686. Sleeping throughout the night only became common within the last 200 years. Before then, people had a first and second sleep, often working, reading or even making love for an hour or so between sleeps.

687. A wealthy man named Howard Lutnick donated more than $65 million to Haverford College because, when he was going there years ago, he lost both of his parents to cancer; however, the college let him go tuition-free for all four years, and that was his way of paying them back.

688. Alexander the First, the king of Yugoslavia, refused to attend public events on Tuesdays after three of his family members died on that day of the week. However, after finally being forced to make an appearance on a Tuesday in October of 1934, he was assassinated.

689. Theophilus Van Kannel invented the revolving doors in 1881. He did so because he hated chivalry, especially the idea of opening doors for women.

690. The petals of a sunflower are actually each single-petalled flowers. The sunflower itself is actually a cluster of hundreds of flowers.

691. Colonel Sanders got fired from dozens of jobs including being a lawyer, and found himself broke at the age of 65. That's when he decided to start KFC.

692. Liam Neeson actually used to be a schoolteacher and did it for two years but got fired for punching a 15-year-old boy in the face when the student pulled a knife out in class.

693. Research gathered at Vienna University concluded that the older a father is when he has a child, the less attractive the child will be.

694. The quickest red card ever given out in soccer history was just three seconds into the match, when player Lee Todd, who played for Chippenham in the U.K., exclaimed, "Eff me, that was loud," after the starting whistle was blown.

695. Back in 2005, there were 71 potential witnesses to a murder in a Belfast bar who all claimed to be in the toilet during the attack. The four-by-three toilets became nicknamed, "The TARDIS."

696. A nine-year-old orphaned child from Rwanda named Justus Uwayesu lived in a garbage dump until American Red Cross workers helped him. Today, he's 23 and is attending Harvard on a full scholarship.

697. A 10-year psychology study undertaken in Germany since the 1980s found that men who kiss their wives before leaving for work lived, on average, five years longer, earned 20-30% more and got into fewer car accidents.

698. There's a Romanian woman who knitted a vest made out of her own hair. She gathered all of the hair that fell out when she combed it from the age of 40 to 60 and eventually had enough hair to produce the article, totalling 2.2 pounds (one kilogram).

699. You can buy toothpaste infused with caffeine that gives you a boost in the morning. Unlike coffee, Power Energy Toothpaste takes effect almost immediately, making you more alert before you're even finished brushing.

700. The oldest inhabited house in Scotland is Traquair Castle. Located less than 30 miles from Edinburgh, it has been lived in for over 900 years and was originally a hunting lodge for the kings and queens of Scotland.

701. There's a mobile game that was released in 2014 titled "Run Forrest Run" that was inspired by the Paramount Pictures 1994 classic, "Forrest Gump," where you literally run through his entire life story.

702. Carrie Fisher wore no underwear in Star Wars because George Lucas convinced her that there were no underwear in outer space.

703. Hopscotch, written by Julio Cortazar, published in 1966, is a 154-chapter-long book that makes sense no matter what chapter you choose to read first or last.

704. In 2015, President Barack Obama personally thanked Japan for karate, karaoke, manga, anime and, of course, emojis.

705. Coffee beans aren't actually beans, they're fruit pits.

706. In 2012, the entire village of Sodeto in Spain won the lottery, except for one man who was never offered a ticket, as those that were selling them forgot to ask him.

707. In 1914, British World War I soldier Thomas Hughes tossed a beer bottle with a letter to his wife into the English Channel, which was discovered in 1999 by a fisherman, who then delivered it to Hughes' 86-year-old daughter.

708. In 2013, a 10-year-old boy named Griffin Sanders from Colorado saved his great-grandmother's life in a speeding vehicle after she fell unconscious. He did this by driving it himself, which he learned by playing Mario Kart.

709. Since the beginning of recorded history, the world has only been at peace for a total of 268 years. That's only 8% of the time.

710. Giraffes only sleep for 30 minutes a day and need the least sleep out of all mammals.

711. Soviet Union leader Joseph Stalin's son, Yakov, was captured while fighting the Nazis in 1941, but Yakov died in captivity because Stalin refused to trade a marshal for a lieutenant.

712. The Mexican drug cartels made a combined estimate of $29 billion in 2010. That's about the same earnings as Google.

713. After the release of Rocky IV, a joke was making its way around Hollywood that, since Rocky had run out of opponents, that he would have to fight an alien in the fifth installment. However, shockingly, screenwriters Jim and John Thomas took the joke seriously and wrote a screenplay based on that joke, which ultimately became the plot for the movie Predator.

714. There are actually some women in the world with four color receptor cells in their eyes, which can allow them to see 100 million colors. To put that into perspective for you, a typical human only has three color receptors and can only see about one million colors.

715. Elephants are one of the only animals who can suffer from post-traumatic stress disorder.

716. Between the 1940s and 1970s, Harvard, Yale, and other Ivy League schools actually took nude photos of each freshman student in an attempt to link physical attributes to intelligence. Notable names include George Bush, Diane Sawyer, Meryl Streep and Hillary Clinton.

717. Researchers have found that for a century female students have consistently earned higher grades than male students. And although fewer women choose to pursue science, technology, engineering and math careers, they excel in these subjects.

718. One penny doubled every day becomes over five million dollars in just thirty days.

719. It takes seventeen muscles to smile and forty-three to frown.

720. In some species of turtles, the temperature determines if the egg will develop into a male or female. Lower temperatures lead to a male, while high temperatures lead to a female.

721. The eyes of a horse can actually move independently. So, it has panoramic vision.

722. Icelanders consume more Coca-Cola per capita than any other nation.

723. The Atlas moth defends itself by imitating a snake's appearance and behavior. Along with convincing wing patterns, the moth will fall to the ground when threatened, and flop around to look like a writhing snake.

724. Andrew Jackson's political opponents referred to him as a 'jackass'. So, he adopted the name and used it as his campaign symbol. It would eventually become the symbol of the entire democratic party in America.

725. Japan now has retirement homes for senior dogs so they can get adequate love and care that they need for their final years.

726. The term, 'swansong', comes from an ancient belief that a swan is silent for its entire life until it sings one beautiful song just before dying.

727. You can actually fix your vision while you sleep. Orthokeratology lenses reshape your corneas overnight so you don't need to wear corrective lenses while you're awake. When you remove them in the morning, you can see just as clearly as you would with prescription lenses.

728. Watermelon contains high levels of vitamin B6, so eating it can actually help relieve stress and anxiety.

729. It is dangerous to feed moose. Moose that are fed by humans become aggressive If the next human doesn't feed them, and may actually end up attacking them.

730. North Korea doesn't have a law against marijuana. In fact people can smoke pot openly in the country and not be criminalized.

731. There's an animal called the Kashmir musk deer or vampire deer that were spotted for the first time in over 60 years in Afghanistan. These creatures are extremely rare because poachers sell their scent glands for more money than gold.

732. People have actually begun putting QR codes on their loved ones gravestones. Scanning them will lead you to online tributes to the dead where you can read their obituaries.

733. The time machine in "Back to the Future" was originally going to be a refrigerator, but was changed when the creators thought kids would trap themselves in fridges while trying to replicate the scene.

734. China is currently constructing the world's longest and highest glass-bottom bridge and it will be over 1400 feet (430 meters) long.

735. Most Dalmatian puppies are born with solid white coats. The spots are invisible until the puppies are about 10 days old.

736. Bulls are actually colorblind. The matador's cape could be any color. It's the motion that attracts the bull's attention to charge, not the color red.

737. Catfish have approximately 100,000 taste buds all over their bodies, most of them on their whiskers.

738. Cranberries are called bounce berries by some people because they actually bounce when they're ripe.

739. Europe is the only continent without at least one desert region. In order to qualify as a desert, an area must get less than 10 inches of rain per year.

740. If you have an irrational fear of Friday the 13th, you have what's called Friggatriskaidekaphobia.

741. According to National Geographic, an elephant's trunk has 150,000 muscle units.

742. Gloucestershire Airport in England used to blast Tina Turner music to scare off birds and it worked better than blasting bird distress calls.

743. The modern Ouija Board got its name in 1890 by asking the board what it should be called. It's spelled out Ouija, and when asked what it meant, the board said, "Good luck."

744. In 2010, an Ikea located in Wembley, England unleashed 100 cats into a store just to see what would happen.

745. Renowned film actress from the 1930's and 50's Hedy Lamarr, was also a mathematician. She was also the inventor of the frequency hopping spread spectrum, a technology still used today for Bluetooth and WiFi.

746. In 2012, a stray cat became a seeing eye-guide for a blind dog named Terfel who uses its paws to gently lead him around the house.

747. Sandy Island located between Australia and New Caledonia was chartered on maps for over a century until a crew of scientists sailed to the location in 2012 and found that it didn't actually exist.

748. If all the world's population, approximately 7.4 billion people, piled into the Grand Canyon, they wouldn't even come close to filling it up.

749. A man once faked mental illness to get out of prison because he thought living in an asylum would be better. However, once he got to the asylum he tried to get out but the doctors actually diagnosed him as a sociopath because faking a mental illness to get out of prison is exactly the type of manipulative behavior you'd expect from a sociopath.

750. Sarpa Salpa is a fish that can cause hallucinations if its head is eaten. It used to be consumed as a recreational drug during the Roman empire.

751. A man in New York named Robert Samuels is a professional line sitter who makes up to $1,000 a week just by standing in line for people.

752. Action gamers are better learners. They excel at predicting the sequence of upcoming events and become better learners by playing fast-paced games.

753. A single share of Coca-Cola stock that was purchased in 1919 for $40, would be worth $9.8 million today.

754. Robert Emmet Odlum, the first person to jump off of the Brooklyn Bridge, was a professional high-diver who wanted to demonstrate that people did not die by simply falling through the air and he proved himself correct by falling 41 meters safely through the air only to die when he hit the water.

755. South Carolina high school student Alex Stone was arrested, suspended, and had his locker searched because of a creative writing assignment where he mentioned buying a gun to shoot his neighbor's pet dinosaur.

756. There's a genetic disease called Laron Syndrome that results in short stature, long life expectancy and near immunity to cancer and diabetes, among other things.

757. In 1942, a British forest guard in India made an alarming discovery when he found at 16,000 feet (4,877 meters) above

sea level, at the bottom of a small valley in a frozen lake, hundreds of unknown skeletons.

758. During Roman times, salt was worth its weight in gold, and soldiers were sometimes paid in salt, hence the word salary.

759. It is impossible for quicksand to suck you under because you simply aren't dense enough to sink in it. However, it liquefies the more you disturb it, as long as you don't panic, you'll only sink about half your body length.

760. There is a Korean eatery in Zhengzhou City, China, known as Zhengzhou Island, where people are allowed to dine at no charge if they happen to be among the five most beautiful patrons of the day.

761. A study from 1978 followed up on 515 people who were prevented from attempting suicide using the Golden Gate Bridge between 1937 and 1971. Ninety percent were either alive, or died of natural causes, with the study concluding that suicidal behaviors are crisis oriented, rather than inexorable.

762. In 2008, it took Apple a year to sell 10 million iPhones. In its first week of sales in 2015, the iPhone 6 sold 13 million units.

763. By law, no U.S. officer's ever allowed to out-rank George Washington, and he was posthumously promoted to history's only six star general in 1976.

764. 'Panda nanny' is a real job position, where you get to spend 365 days a year with panda babies for an annual salary of 32 thousand dollars.

765. The platypus has no nipples and milk simply oozes from their skin.

766. When a coal mine catches fire it can burn for decades or even centuries. There are thousands of these fires across the world.

767. Believe it or not, socks are among the most needed items at homeless shelters, yet among the least often donated.

768. A dog named Greyfriars Bobby in Scotland sat by his owner's grave for 14 years until he eventually passed away.

769. An anonymous sent thousands of all black faxes to the Church of Scientology to deplete all of their ink cartridges.

770. All new employees and recently promoted executives at the Japanese company, Dentsu, have to climb Mount Fuji. This has happened every July since 1925.

771. The horse head used in The Godfather was a real horse head, not a prop. John Marley was not informed beforehand, so his scream was authentic, not scripted.

772. Momentary Ink, prints your tattoo designs as customary, temporary tattoos that last 3-10 days so that you can try out your ideas before you commit to one.

773. Glass is 100% recyclable and it can be recycled endlessly without loss in quality or purity.

774. You can have brain surgery and not feel any pain because the brain itself does not have any pain receptors.

775. Silbury Hill near Avebury in Wiltshire, England, is the largest prehistoric man-made mound in Europe. It stands 130 feet (40 meters) high, and its purpose is still unknown.

776. The diameter of the planet Uranus is 31,763 miles (9400 meters) across. That's four times bigger than earth.

777. The Vatican has its own soccer team. Vatican City is the smallest independent state in the world, and therefore has its own national soccer team or, as they call it in Europe, football team.

778. From 2012 to 2015 how to kiss was the most popular how to search on YouTube. That was followed by how to tie a tie, how to draw and how to get a six pack in three minutes.

779. There are parts of the Atacama Desert in Chile that have not seen a drop of water since record keeping began.

780. The Milky Way has between 100 and 400 billion stars, but we can only see about 2,500 of them at any one point from the globe since our solar system resides roughly 27,000 light years away from the galactic center.

781. Historians believe that William Shakespeare was born and died on the same date. He was born on April 23, 1564 and he died on April 23, 1616.

782. In 2001 and 2002, Argentina had five presidents in two weeks. the string of presidents started when Fernando de la Rua

resigned in December of 2001. The last of the five was appointed in January of 2002 amid major protesting.

783. Googling 'do a barrel roll' makes your whole browser flip over.

784. Amish men are actually clean shaven prior to getting married but are required to grow their beards after marriage. This and all aspects of Amish life are dictated by a list of written and oral rules known as Ordnung, which outlines the basics of the Amish faith and helps to define what it means to be Amish.

785. In 2015, a man who skipped out on his bill at a Houston area restaurant was seen running into a vacant building across the street. The police officers who arrived jokingly called out "Marco" to which the suspect accidentally replied, "Polo." He was immediately arrested.

786. Believe it or not it's possible to donate your voice. There's an organization called vocal ID that encourages people to donate their voices so that they can recreate synthetic voices that are just as unique as fingerprints to suit individuals who have speech impairments.

787. Only three humans have ever died outside of the Earth's atmosphere. They were all on the Soyuz 11 the only manned mission to board the world's first space station which ended in disaster when the crew capsule depressurized.

788. Edward Jones or Boy Jones was known in the Victorian era for getting caught breaking into Buckingham Palace when he was 14 years old and stealing Queen Victoria's underwear.

789. Billboards have been banned in Vermont since 1968 in order to preserve the natural beauty of the state.

790. The Goliath tigerfish is the largest of the tigerfish clan and can be found in the Congo River Basin. In fact it's so big it's been known to eat small crocodiles and has even attacked humans on several instances.

791. A recent study found that a 45 to 60 minute nap during the day could improve learning and memory by as much as five fold. Researchers say that a short nap at the office or in school is enough to improve learning success.

792. The Chinese government takes its officials and members of their families on prison tours to give them an introduction to what awaits them if they should engage in corruption.

793. In 1972, the king of Morocco, Hassan the Second, grabbed the radio during an assassination attempt and told the rebel pilots who were firing at him inside his Boeing 727 to stop firing the tyrant is dead, which made the assassins break off from their attempt.

794. When you kiss someone for the first time, you get a spike in the neurotransmitter Dopamine making you crave more. Endorphins are also released bringing on waves of euphoria.

795. Sadie Renee Johnson from Oregon started a wildfire in 2013 in order to give her bored firefighter friends some work, except that it spread to 206 square kilometers and cost nearly eight million dollars and two months to bring under control.

796. In 2015, a stray cat in Russia known as Masha kept a two-month-old abandoned baby boy warm in freezing temperatures overnight.

797. Jerusalem is one of the oldest cities in the world. It has been destroyed twice, besieged 23 times, captured, and then re-captured 44 times, and attacked a total of 52 times.

798. In 1915, a millionaire named, Cecil Chubb bought his wife Stonehenge for approximately 10,000 dollars. Except that, she didn't like it, so in 1918 he gave it to Britain and today it's valued at around 51 million dollars.

799. In the traditional aboriginal Canadian version of lacrosse, teams consisted of 100 to 1,000 men and fields were 500 meters to three kilometers long. Games could last up to three days straight.

800. Research conducted by the University of Exeter concluded that every individual shark has its own distinct character and personality. Some sharks are shy, while others are more social.

801. Billionaire Elon Musk didn't like the school that his kids were attending, so he conceptualized and built his own named Ad Astra, which means 'to the stars'.

802. The SR 71 Blackbird was the world's fastest air breeding man-made aircraft and out ran nearly 4,000 missiles fired at it during its service.

803. When syphilis first surfaced, most countries named it after one another. The English called it the French disease. The French called it the Spanish disease, and the Japanese called it the Chinese Pox.

804. In the late 1800's, archaeologists found a ring inside a ninth-century Viking grave in Sweden inscribed with the phrase, "For Allah". This linked trade between Swedish Vikings and the Islamic world all the way back to 1,000 years ago.

805. According to the Centers For Disease Control And Prevention, on average people who smoke die 10 years earlier than non-smokers. And every person who dies because of smoking, at least 30% of people live with a serious smoking related illness.

806. Jell-O is made from gelatin that is produced by boiling the bones, skin, and hides of animals such as cows and pigs. People have been eating it since 1897, and it accounts for about 80% of the gelatin market.

807. Abraham Lincoln was in the National Wrestling Hall of Fame. He had an awesome physical size at six foot four, was widely known for his wrestling skills, and had only one reported defeat in a dozen years.

808. Echidnas have a four-headed penis. Also known as spiny anteaters; they don't even use their penis to urinate and it only leaves the body during an erection.

809. The Golden Silk Orb Weave spider's web is so strong that it can capture a bird, of which the spider then eats.

810. Marigolds and other plants that contain the pigment Xanthophyll are added to chicken feed to make their egg yolks appear more orange.

811. In Peru, fried or roasted guinea pig is considered a delicacy. Known as cuy, it's been a staple in Peru's diet for around 5,000 years.

812. The Aztec people often used cocoa beans as currency.

813. Argyria is a condition which turns a person's skin a bright blue color. It's caused by chronic exposure to silver.

814. In 1998, construction worker Travis Bogumill was accidentally shot with a nail gun that drove a 3.25-inch nail into his skull. The nail lodged in the area of the brain that typically involves processing math. He was completely fine after the nail was removed, except his math skills weren't what they used to be.

815. In the year 1900, inventor Ludwig Ederer invented an alarm mechanism that was built into your bed. When you set the alarm to a specific time, the bed rose to a 45-degree angle and tipped you out of bed.

816. Murder rates were so high during the 1970's and 1980's in Miami, Florida, that the Dade County Medical Examiner's office actually had to rent a refrigerated trailer from Burger King to handle the overflow of corpses.

817. After the Fukushima nuclear disaster in 2011, more than 200 Japanese pensioners all over volunteered to tackle the nuclear crisis.

818. Research conducted by psychologists at Bernell University determined that those who use Facebook to brag about diets and exercise, and accomplishments, are typically narcissists.

819. There exists a special shaped knife for cleaning out Nutella jars entirely.

820. Sir Richard Branson once lost a bet with AirAsia's CEO, Tony Fernandes, on the winner of the 2010 Grand Prix in Abu Dhabi. He had to work as a female flight attendant on Tony's airline.

821. When your eyes move, your brain purposely blocks your vision, which is why you can't see the motion of your own eyes in a mirror. This is called 'saccadic masking' and without it, your life would be like watching a movie that's filled with a shaky hand-held camera.

822. When Steven Spielberg first applied to USC Cinematic Art School, he was rejected three times by the admissions officer. When Steven was awarded his honorary doctorate from that

school, he agreed to accept it, only if it was personally signed by that same admissions officer, and it was.

823. A man named Chito, rescued a dying crocodile, who named it Pocho, but it recovered and refused to leave the man's side, and they are inseparable to this day.

824. In ancient Egypt, little people were seen as people with celestial gifts, and they were treated like Gods and given the highest social positions.

825. Michael Nicholson, a man from Michigan, has one bachelor's degree, two associates' degrees, and 22 master's degrees, 3 specialist's degrees, and one doctoral degree, making him the most credentialed person in history.

826. Cheetah cubs have long, tall hairs that run from their neck, all the way down to the base of their tail, called mantle. It makes a cheetah cub look like a honey badger and makes them blend into the tall grass keeping them from threats, like lions and hyenas.

827. Native American people intentionally bent trees to mark trails, and many remain today as hidden monuments.

828. A millionaire Chinese businessman named Xiong Shuihua, decided to bulldoze entire rundown huts in his village where he grew up and decided to build luxury flats, then gave the keys to the residents instead, for free.

829. Happier cows really do produce more milk, and simply calling cows by individual names ups production by 3.5 percent.

830. The skull that Russians kept as evidence of Hitler's death is actually the skull of a woman.

831. Caterpillars completely turn to liquid in a cocoon, but as a moth/butterfly can still remember their life as a caterpillar.

832. The steamboat Arabia, which sank in 1856, was excavated in 1988 under almost 14 meters of dirt in a field at a farm. Interestingly many artifacts were recovered and preserved so well that some of the food was actually still edible.

833. Diana Kim, a photographer from Hawaii, who after 10 years documenting the homeless, found her own father among them.

834. Wildlife photographer Alan McFadyen spent 42 hundred hours and took 720 thousand photos, over a six-year period before he finally got the perfect shot of a Kingfisher diving into water without making a splash.

835. Owning a hamster, gerbil, or ferret is illegal in Hawaii. You're also not allowed to own an alligator, a piranha, or a toucan either.

836. In 2013, Ben and Jerry's received the Compassion in World Farming's Good Dairy award for their high quality treatment of their cows, which includes making sure that they get regular massages. They also pay their employees double minimum wage.

837. There's an area in France covering 39 square miles known as Zone Rouge. It's so polluted with unexploded chemical munitions, human and animal remains from both World Wars, humans are prohibited by law from entering that area.

838. There's a ghost town in Tianducheng, China that was built in 2007 that looks just like Paris. It includes a 354 foot replica of the Eiffel Tower. They also have replica Italian, German, and English towns, but they too are ghost towns.

839. In 2006, a group of researchers in Iceland found a really old clam. In order to find out its age, instead of counting the rings on the outside of the clam, they opened it and counted the rings on the inside, ultimately killing the clam. The clam itself ended up being 507 years old, one of the world's oldest animals.

840. In 2014 Japanese designer Akiro Mizuchi created edible chocolate Legos that were actually functional.

841. The pound key on your keyboard, or 'hashtag' as you know it, is called an octotroph.

842. Budokan or Otakon was known as the Mayan god of wind and storms. His name means one-legged in the Mayan language, and the word hurricane was derived from his name.

843. There is a twitter account called big _ben_clock and it tweets bong bong bong-bong-bong every hour. It's been doing this since 2009.

844. Sandwiches taste better when someone else makes them. A psychologist named Daniel Kahneman explains that this is because when we make our own sandwiches, we anticipate their taste and therefore pre consume them and therefore are less hungry afterwards.

845. Interestingly blood has similar properties to eggs in cooking and can actually be used as a viable substitute in baking.

846. In 2015, a passenger on British Airways took a poop that smelled so bad that pilots actually decided to turn the plane around.

847. The reflex that causes people to sneeze when looking at the sun is called the "photic sneeze reflex". It's also known as Autosomal Dominant Compelling Helio-ophthalmic Outburst Syndrome, which abbreviates to ADCHOO.

848. A pine tree planted in 2004 in Los Angeles Park in memory of former Beatle, George Harrison, died after being infested by beetles.

849. Studies have shown that when a woman frequently texts her partner in a relationship, they are both happier with each other. However, when a man sends the majority of texts, both partners feel less happy and a woman often considers ending the relationship.

850. A German officer once asked Picasso, "Did you do this?" when he saw a photo of the painting Guernica, a painting about the effect of German bombardment on the Spanish town of Guernica, to which, Picasso simply responded, "No, you did."

851. There is an Asian elephant named Koshik that can imitate human speech by sticking it's trunk in its mouth. He can actually say, 'Hello', 'good', 'no', 'sit down', and 'lie down' in Korean.

852. We actually have the ability to eat an entire bag of chips without really noticing, because chips have a vanishing caloric density. What that means is that it tricks our tongue and brain into thinking that we haven't actually eaten anything.

853. Famed artist Bob Ross painted a grayscale landscape in 1984 after meeting a colorblind man who believed that he would never be able to paint to show him that he can.

854. The eye color of owls typically indicates what time of day the owls prefer to be active and hunt. Their eyes can be yellow, orange, dark brown, or even black.

855. Ancient Babylonians took beer brewing extremely seriously. Anyone found brewing bad beer was punished in one of two ways; death by drowning in that barrel of beer or by drinking their crappy beer until they died.

856. Tokyo has its own superhero. His name is Mangetsu Man, a self-made hero who's taken up the responsibility of keeping the city clean. He wears a full moon head, purple bodysuit, oversized Ugg boots, with matching gloves, and uses a voice dictation app to hide his voice.

857. Researchers from the University of Michigan have found a way to allow people to have vision at night. In 2014, they developed a graphene contact lens that allows users to change the kind of light that they see.

858. A company in Singapore made a pair of soft drinks called Anything and Whatever. The two lines of drinks had six flavors each but both had generic packaging designs so there was no way to tell what flavor was in each can.

859. Kamala Devi, a 56 year old Indian woman, was ambushed by a leopard and actually managed to kill it with the only thing that she had on her, an iron sickle.

860. For the film, 'Gone Girl', David Fincher wanted Ben Affleck to wear a Yankees cap for a scene. Affleck, a diehard Red Sox fan, adamantly refused, and this led to a four-day production halt until the two came to an agreement that he would wear a Mets cap.

861. In the 1800s, researchers found one of the first ever iron maidens in a castle in Nuremberg, Germany. An iron maiden is a device of torture where the person is put inside a sarcophagus with spikes on the inner surface. When the doors were closed, the spikes would puncture several organs, including their eyes, but not deep enough to kill them, just deep enough that they would bleed to death over several hours.

862. Yahoo was originally called Jerry's Guide to the World Wide Web after one of its creators, Jerry Yang.

863. In 1881, dentist Alfred Southwick got the idea for the electric chair after witnessing a freak accident when an intoxicated man died after he accidentally touched a live generator terminal.

864. The barreleye fish has a completely transparent head. It inhabits depths of around 2,000 feet (600 meters) to 2,600 feet (800 meters) where the darkness approaches absolute black.

865. Some insects smell with their genitalia. There's a genetic disease called fish odor syndrome where a person excretes an excess of chemicals called TMA in the urine, sweat, and breath that causes them to smell like rotting fish.

866. The average person has two million sweat glands.

867. The parliament of Iceland is the oldest still-acting parliament in the world. It was founded back in 930 A.D. Political gatherings typically lasted for two weeks in June, which was a period of uninterrupted daylight and nice weather.

868. The Maya found slightly crossed eyes beautiful. Parents of babies would actually hang objects like stones right between their baby's eyes to try to get them to go cross-eyed.

869. Lyme disease got its name because it was first recognized back in 1975 when researchers found that a large number of children in Lyme, Connecticut were being diagnosed with juvenile rheumatoid arthritis.

870. A group of porcupines is called a prickle.

871. D-day was originally set for June fifth, but had to be postponed for 24 hours due to bad weather.

872. The green ink used in American money was actually invented at McGill University in Montreal, Canada in 1857 by Thomas Dairy Hunt.

873. A team of archaeologists found what they believe to be the world's oldest board game in a 5,000-year-old bronze age burial site in Turkey. They believe that board games originated in Egypt in the Fertile Crescent.

874. The Tumbler for the Dark Knight trilogy is actually a working vehicle, not a CGI model.

875. The most expensive guitar pick costs, $4,674 and is made out of a meteor. It's made by the company, Star Picks.

876. There's a UK based company named 'Gumdrop' that recycles gum into bins that are made out of entirely recycled gum.

877. There is a territory in Costa Rica called Territorio De Zaguates, which means land of the strays, which is basically a huge no-kill dog shelter where you can hike for free with dogs.

878. On November 7th, 1907, a Mexican railroad worker called Jesus Garcia single-handedly saved the population of a nearby town called Nacozari Sonora by driving a train loaded with dynamite away. The train exploded six kilometers away from the town and killed the brave man in the process.

879. To burn off 200 calories, you could chew gum for 18 hours, apply lip balm 1500 times, or sing a song 23 times.

880. Planes used to be a lot more comfortable. In the 1940s, the Boeing 377 Stratocruiser had reclining club chairs throughout the cabin. On intercontinental flights, every seat could adjust into a bed so that each passenger could sleep.

881. Raccoons are actually very smart. They can open complex locks in under 10 tries and can still repeat the process if the locks are rearranged or turned upside down. They'll also remember solutions to problems for up to three years.

882. Former two time heavyweight champion, George Foreman, is now the pastor of North Houston's Church of the Lord Jesus Christ. The 68 year old reverend was inspired to join the church as he himself grew up in poverty and wanted to help others after a successful career.

883. In January of 1966, the U.S. accidentally bombed Spain. An Air Force bomber carrying four nuclear weapons collided with its refueling tanker over the Spanish town of Palomares, sending the bombs screaming towards earth.

884. ESPN, the sports television channel is actually owned by Disney with a majority ownership of 80% but that's not all. Disney also

owns Pixar, Lucasfilm, Marvel, ABC Broadcasting Company and A&E, as well as the History Channel.

885. In 2015, Japan lifted its 67 year old ban on dancing that it put in place after World War II. They forbade dancing in venues without a special dance license. The law was originally put into place after the second World War in an effort to crack down on dance halls that were often a hot spot for prostitution.

886. If you feel strongly that someone is watching you, that's because they probably are. Your brain has a primal gaze detection system that determines whether someone is staring directly at you or not.

887. Clinical studies done at Stanford University show that people who have auditory hallucinations, such as schizophrenia, have voices that are shaped by cultural influences. In Africa and India, most describe them as voices of family members or spirits, but most Americans say that they hear violent, torturous, and hateful yelling from strangers.

888. There are actually 3D printers that can print your dinner. The Foodini Food Printer makes everything from pizza to burgers to chocolate using fresh ingredients.

889. A free kitchen, operated by volunteers in India at the Golden Temple in the Western Indian City of Amritsar serves 100,000 hot meals a day and has been doing so for over 300 years.

890. The average claw machine is only programmed to give the claw full strength every 20 tries.

891. Basma Hameed, a Canadian woman originally from Iraq, learned how to tattoo so that she could cover her burn scars that she received on her face as a child. The results were remarkable and she now has a business helping other burn victims by tattooing discolored scars to match their own skin tone.

892. There exists an American company known as "Creative Home Engineering" that specializes in making hidden rooms for your home. There's even one that requires a chess board played in a certain combination in order to unlock the room.

893. The United Kingdom and Portugal hold the longest standing alliance in the world which started 1386 years ago.

894. Born in the 1930s, identical twins Oskar Stohr and Jack Yufe were separated shortly after birth. Oskar was raised in Germany and attended Hitler Youth Academy while Jack practiced Judaism in Trinidad. They finally met at the age of 21 and they didn't get along at first, but eventually became close brothers later in their 50s.

895. When a cat brings back a dead animal, it's actually acting out its natural role as a mother and teaching, showing its owners how to catch and eat prey, just like they would teach their young in the wild.

896. Your blood actually appears green underwater at about nine meters or so because there is no red light under water, therefore, there is no red light that can bounce off of your blood into our eyes.

897. In 2012, following the death of 'Meow', a cat who weighed 18 kilograms, the Guinness Book of World Records stopped recording the heaviest pets in the world to discourage deliberate overeating.

898. You can differentiate between East from West Berlin from space because the different types of street lamps used to give off different shades of light.

899. Jerome Rodale, a longevity expert and father of organic farming announced at the age of 71, during an interview that he's decided to live to be 100. He also declared, "I've never felt better in my life." and minutes later, while filming, he died of a heart attack.

900. There is a boiling lake located in Dominica that is so hot, the centers temperature has never been determined.

901. The Grasshopper mouse is carnivorous, immune to venom, eats scorpions, and howls like a wolf to claim its territory.

902. The Spanish Paralympic basketball team was forced to return the gold medals that they won in the 2000 Australian Paralympics after almost all players were found to be not disabled.

903. Some non-venomous snakes, like the Tiger Keelback, will actually protect their babies by eating poisonous frogs while

being pregnant. They then pass the poison onto their eggs which makes their newborns poisonous when they're born.

904. On December 31st, 1946, a man named Alphonse Rocco claimed to be a detective and gave a pedestrian a camera and asked her to take a picture of a suspect. The detective turned out to be a gangster and the suspect turned out to be his ex-wife and the camera turned out to be a concealed shotgun, firing via the shutter button.

905. In Bridgeport, in the UK, there is a cat named the Artful Dodger who regularly catches the bus by himself to travel 10 miles to the neighboring town. He waits at the bus stop so often that the driver brings tins of cat food and knows what stop to let the cat off at.

906. Dr. Seuss' first book was rejected 27 times. He was almost ready to give up but bumped into a friend on the street in New York City back in 1937 who had just begun working in publishing. Seuss said that if he had been walking on the other side of the street, he probably would have never been a children's author.

907. Scaphism was a form of ancient punishment where the victim was tied and force fed a rich diet of honey and milk and then left in the sun. He accumulated diarrhea while his excretion attracted flies and insects who would then eventually eat the man inside out.

908. In September of 1940, two planes collided over Brocklesby, Australia, and interlocked the engines of the plane on top which stopped working. The ones on the plane underneath continued to work however and the pilot of that plane landed both planes safely and all four crewmen survived.

909. Kim jong-nam is Kim Jong un's older brother and was supposed to be Kim Jong Il's successor. However, he fell out of the line of succession when he tried to fake a passport so that he could get into Disneyland in Japan.

910. Japanese engineer Kuniako Saito invented a new, tiny, personal transportation system, the "WalkCar", similar to an electric skateboard, but small enough to fit right in your backpack.

911. The world record for the largest number ever counted belongs to Jeremy Harper. He streamlined the entire process online and raised money for charity. He reached one million. It took him three months.

912. The first guest to enter Disneyland was college student Dave MacPherson. He didn't ride a single attraction because he had to get back to school. He was awarded a lifelong ticket to Disneyland, with up to three guests, and the ticket has since been extended to include Disney parks around the world.

913. Norwegian student Kristoffer Koch spent 27 dollars on bitcoins, forgot about them, and then years later realized they were worth 886 thousand dollars.

914. Inmates at a Bolivia prison live as a society. They have jobs, buy or rent their accommodation and often live with their families.

915. There's a fish called the black dragon fish that looks like the creature from the Alien movies.

916. In 1994, a 34-kilogram bag of cocaine fell out of a plane and landed in the middle of a Florida crime watch meeting.

917. A Chinese millionaire began selling cans of fresh air for 80 cents a can in response to China's worsening air pollution and made over $6 million.

918. It is in fact possible to find DNA traces from cigarette butts. An artist named Heather Dewey Hagboard used cigarette butts and old chewing gum that she found thrown away on the streets to create 3d portraits of people whose DNA was found on those objects.

919. Naturally purple eyes exist and this is due to a disorder called Alexandria's Genesis which causes pale skin and purple eyes.

920. Despite being much smaller in size, the Wolverine can successfully attack much larger animals including caribous and elk.

921. Residents of the village of Shitterton in England, grew so tired of people stealing a sign with the village name on it, that they replaced it with a 1.5-ton block of stone with the village name inscribed upon it.

922. There are pink bananas that exist called Musa velutina, and they peel themselves when ripe. They're often grown as an ornamental, but have soft sweet flesh and can be eaten. The seeds however are quite hard and can chip a tooth.

923. According to research our voices change when we find people attractive. These vocal modulations tend to be subtle and the speaker usually isn't conscious of the change.

924. The world record for the most passengers carried on a commercial aircraft was set on May 24th, 1991 when over 1000 Ethiopian Jews were evacuated to Israel. The flight started with 1086 people in the plane but ended with 1088 people because two of them had babies on route to Israel.

925. The African grey parrot, N'kisi, has a whopping 950 word vocabulary that even impressed the famous primatologist Jane Goodall. N'kisi has seen photos of her, and when they met asked "got a chimp?"

926. In 2002, an unnamed Croatian diver got lost in an underwater cave, and stabbed himself in the chest to avoid the agony of drowning. It was the first documented case of someone committing suicide while diving.

927. In medieval Germany, married couples could legally settle their disputes by fighting a marital duel. To even the field, the men had to fight from inside a hole with one arm tied behind his back. The woman was free to move and armed with a sack full of rocks.

928. The Soviet tenor, Victor Ivanovich Nikitin, was so good that when he sang to Soviet troops at the east from World War II, German troops on the other side stopped shooting just to listen.

929. In 2001, a lion cub, bear cub, and tiger cub were found neglected in a drug dealer's basement, but they have lived together ever since they were adopted by a sanctuary, and are considered inseparable because of the strong friendship that they have.

930. There's a guitar shaped forest in Argentina. The 7,000 trees were planted by a farmer named Pedro Martin Ureta. He planted them in 1979 as a tribute to his late wife. He's never been able to see it himself from above, because he's terrified of flying.

931. A third grade girl was expelled for a year because her grandmother sent her a birthday cake to school along with a knife to cut it. The teacher used the knife to cut the cake, and then reported the girl to the authorities for having a dangerous weapon.

932. A man in Saudi Arabia installed a community fridge outside of his home and his neighbor's to donate any extra food that they have, so that those in need could get something to eat without having to beg for it.

933. Self-discipline better predicts success than IQ.

934. According to research done by scientists, in order to lose 63 pounds for his role in The Machinist, Christian Bale's daily diet consisted of one can of tuna fish and/or one apple per day, black coffee, and water.

935. The scientific name for brain freeze is actually sphenopalatine ganglioneuralgia. Brain freezes happen because the cold dilates arteries which causes a sudden rush of blood to the brain, which causes pressure and causes pain.

936. Rabbits actually have the ability to sleep with their eyes open. They go into a trance-like state, which is half asleep. The benefit of this is in the wild, it allows them to get away from predators in a hurry.

937. According to Lita Proctor, the Program Coordinator of the National Institute of Health's Human Microbiome Project, we have enough bacteria in our bodies to fill a large soup can. That's up to five pounds of bacteria.

938. The colossal squid has the largest eyes ever studied in the animal kingdom, measuring almost 11 inches, which is roughly the same size as a volleyball. In fact, researchers believe that they may be the largest eyes that ever existed.

939. Some sharks can live up to 100 years old. Although most of them live 20 to 30 years in the wild, while some species such as the spiny dogfish live well beyond 100 years.

940. Cats actually sweat through their paws. Cats do have sweat glands, but their skin is covered in fur, so the amount of cooling

that the sweat can provide them is minimal. The paw pads have the most sweat glands, so they sweat there mostly.

941. Researchers in the UK have created a robotic rectum for proctologists to practice their physical rectal exams. It allows medical professions to learn without the use of real life volunteers.

942. The tree that owns itself is a white oak tree in Athens, Georgia, that is widely assumed to be legally owned by itself, and eight feet of land surrounding it. According to newspapers, a deed written by Colonel William Jackson, was written to the tree, giving ownership of the land to itself in the 1800's.

943. A man named Nigel Richards from Malaysia, memorized the French dictionary to win the French Scrabble championship, and he doesn't even speak French.

944. One of the top-five things that people regret when they're dying is working too hard and missing out on family time.

945. A 20-year-old anonymous British man from Birmingham dresses up as Spiderman in the night to help homeless people by buying them food from the supermarket.

946. Potoos are a type of bird that uses body posture to camouflage themselves to look like the part of a tree stump.

947. Baby elephants will suck on their trunks for comfort just like human babies suck on their thumbs.

948. Designer Alexander McQueen's former apprentice, Emma Sandham-King, made the world's first Harris tweed suit designed for a horse to celebrate the 2016 Cheltenham Festival. It took four weeks and more than 18 meters of tweed to complete the three-piece suit, which was worn by a racehorse named Morestead.

949. There was a newborn baby that was abandoned in a forest in Kenya for two days back in 2005, that was rescued by a stray dog who carried the baby all the way back to her own litter of puppies.

950. There is a subspecies of butterfly known as the "8998 butterfly". It's named this way for its markings, which uncannily resemble the number 89 on one wing, and the number 98 on the other.

951. In 1896, the world's first speeding ticket was given to a Britain man that was going four times the speeding limit. Walter Arnold, who was going eight miles per hour in a two mile per hour zone was caught by a policeman on a bicycle, and was fined one shilling, which was about eight U.S. cents.

952. Shark teeth are coated with fluoride which acts like toothpaste and keeps the shark's mouth healthy and clean.

953. To punish tree thieves who cut down trees illegally, some cities spray trees with fox urine around Christmas time. It freezes on them and is odorless outdoors, but would stink up your whole house if you brought it indoors. The smell is apparently eye-watering.

954. Some restaurants in China actually lace their food with opiates to keep customers coming back.

955. The Hanover Country School Board in Virginia tried to ban 'To Kill A Mockingbird' in 1966. When she heard about this, author Harper Lee sent a letter to the school board asking if they were literate and offered some money to enroll them in first grade.

956. In 2012 a man named Robert Biggs was attacked by a mountain lion while he was out hiking. Unbelievably a bear saved his life by attacking the lion and driving it away.

957. In 2014 Margaret Loughry won the Northern Ireland lottery jackpot which consisted of 46 million dollars. She donated 44 million of it to her own hometown to help transform it into a tourist destination.

958. Video games can be good for children with autism because it helps them practice skills like self-awareness flexibility and self-control.

959. Honey bees have five eyes, two compound eyes that help them see around themselves, simultaneously, and three simple eyes that are positioned on the top of their heads that help with its orientation.

960. After winning the 2014 FIFA World Cup, German footballer Midget Ozel, donated his 300,000 euro victory bonus to help support 23 Brazilian kids' surgery operations.

961. At the center of every single raindrop is a mineral dust particle, as it is physically impossible for raindrops to form from pure water alone.

962. There is a small village in Holland known as "Dementia Village", inhabited by those people with dementia. It's designed to be a normal environment with a secure perimeter so that patients can safely roam to the grocery store, restaurants, cafes, and gardens.

963. A Stanford study concluded that there is a high correlation between walking and creative thought output. Compared to sitting, those who walked demonstrated a 60% increase in creative thought output.

964. Snapchat founder Evan Spiegel's net worth was $1.5 billion at the age of only 24 making him one of the world's youngest billionaires.

965. Kowloon Walled City in China existed from 1810 to 1993. In its later years, it was controlled by triads with thousands of residents who were involved in drugs, gambling, and prostitution before the city was demolished.

966. Rajendra Singh, known as the water man of India, revived five rivers and brought water back to 1000 villages in India using native water preservation techniques.

967. The pyramids of Giza were more ancient to the ancient Romans than Rome is ancient to us.

968. Gobekli Tepe, located in Turkey, is thought to be the world's oldest temple. Constructed 6000 years before Stonehenge, it's estimated to have been built before the invention of the wheel, even the idea of farming, or the tools that could have constructed its own existence. Basically, it shouldn't have existed itself.

969. When Apple began designating employee numbers, Steve Jobs was offended that Steve Wozniak received number one while he only got number two. He believed that he should be second to no one, so he took number zero instead.

970. In 2015, Apple recovered 2, 200 pounds (1 tonne) of gold from recycled iPhones, iPads, and Macs. That's worth over $40 million. Gold is frequently used in consumer electronics because it's highly averse to corrosion and an excellent conductor of electricity. While silver is actually the best conductor, it corrodes more easily.

971. In ancient Olympics, women were not allowed to compete, and married women weren't even allowed to be in the stands to watch. Only young women and virgins were permitted. Fathers brought their daughters in hopes that they would marry one of the champions.

972. Brazilian police on Marajo Island ride water buffalo when they patrol instead of horses.

973. All Starbucks coffee shops in Saudi Arabia have a gender wall. It separates single men from women and families.

974. Most Bolivian families have a dried llama fetus under the foundation of their houses for luck. They're most commonly found in Bolivia's witches' market where you can also find toad talismans, owl feathers, and stone amulets.

975. Austrian inventor Valentin Vodev has invented a scooter slash stroller hybrid. With the click of a button, the stroller transforms into a scooter and can travel as fast as 10 miles (16 km) per hour.

976. The coconut crab grows over three feet long and is not only the largest land crab but is also the largest arthropod, the group that includes insects, spiders, and crustaceans.

977. Most meteors are actually the size of a grain of sand and disintegrate in the air. The larger ones that actually reach the Earth are called meteorites and are very rare.

978. Believe it or not, green bell peppers are just less mature, less ripe versions of red, orange, and yellow peppers.

979. Back in 2007, a priest was arrested for stalking late night talk show host Conan O'Brien. He was writing threatening notes on parish letterhead, contacting his parents, and showing up at his studio.

980. The stop sign originated in Detroit, Michigan, back in 1915 and was originally black lettering on a white background. Then it was black lettering on a yellow background before it was finally red and white.

981. Hippopotomonstrosesquippedaliophobia means the morbid fear of long words.

982. Jupiter is the fourth-brightest object in our solar system. Only the sun, moon, and Venus are brighter. It is one of the five planets that you can see from Earth with the naked eye.

983. Most predators have eyes facing forward, while most prey have eyes on their sides of their head.

984. Every single restaurant that has appeared on season two of Kitchen Nightmares has closed.

985. In 2013, a man threatening to jump from the South Carolina Ravenel Bridge was convinced not to jump after being offered a pizza.

986. Studies conducted at Indiana University Media School discovered that watching cat videos actually boosts viewer's energy and positive emotions and decreases negative feelings.

987. Smart people underestimate themselves while ignorant people think they're brilliant. It's a cognitive bias called the Dunning-Kruger Effect. It's where the highly-skilled assume that things that they find easy are also easy for others and that the unskilled are so incompetent that they can't recognize their own stupidity.

988. In 2000, cigarette giant Phillip Morris introduced fire-safe cigarettes which actually posed a greater risk of starting fires when left unattended.

989. Prairie dogs have a complex means of communication. It's so advanced that not only do they have different calls depending on the type of predator, but they also make sentences that describe the predator.

990. The concept of rap-battle has existed since the 5th century, where poets would engage in "flighting", which was a spoken

word event where poets would actually insult one another in verse.

991. There are red bananas that taste sweet, creamy, and a little bit like raspberries.

992. Singapore is the only country in the history of the modern world to gain independence against its own will.

993. Cold showers are actually healthier than hot ones. Among other benefits they improve immunity and circulation, ease stress and relieve depression.

994. TashiroJima is an island in Japan that's also known as Cat Island. The stray cat population there is larger than the human population.

995. Scientists at Junagadh University in India have extracted gold from the urine of rare indigenous breeds of cattle. They analyzed 400 Gir cows and found traces of ionized gold salts that they were able to isolate, precipitate, extract, solidify and melt between three to 10 milligrams of gold per liter of urine.

996. Skunks are actually immune to snake venom.

997. The first occurrence of identical bird twins ever was discovered in the emu.

998. Bears are the only mammals that don't pee or poo during the winter hibernation months, and doctors have actually studied how the bears recycle their urine to help human patients with kidney failure.

999. Both Demi Lovato and Selena Gomez were on the TV show Barney and Friends when they were kids. In fact, the long-time friends were constantly shown together dancing and singing on screen.

1000. There is a knife and fork hybrid that exists called a nork.

1001. The air quality in Beijing got so bad in December of 2015 that schools were closed, car travel was restricted, and barbecuing was banned.

1002. Japanese death row inmates aren't told the date of their execution, therefore they wake up every single day wondering if today may be their last.

1003. The Sacramento Public Library started a Library of Things earlier in 2016 which allowed patrons to check out, among other things, sewing machines and other items that patrons may find useful but may not need to own long term.

1004. When the world's top soccer player Cristiano Ronaldo was asked to donate his cleats for a charity auction benefiting 10 month old Erik Ortiz Cruz who had a brain disorder that could cause 30 seizures a day he instead paid the whole $83,000 for his surgery himself.

1005. Bicultural people may change their personality when they switch languages. According to a study conducted by university professors across America, language unconsciously affects people's interpretation of events. Women speaking Spanish were seen as more independent and assertive than women speaking English in similar situations.

1006. Black Panthers are not a real species. What they are, are jaguars and leopards who have 'Melanism', which causes them to have black skin. It's actually the opposite effect of having albinism.

1007. Conservationists in South Africa are infusing a special red dye into the horns of live rhinos. The mixture renders the horn completely useless to poachers that are trying to sell it commercially and also has a toxin for human consumption.

1008. President Andrew Jackson's pet parrot was kicked out of Jackson's funeral in 1945 for cursing.

1009. In 30 seconds, you will on average, produce 72 million red blood cells, shed 174,000 skin cells and have 25 thoughts.

1010. In 2014, a stray dog named Arthur followed a Swedish racing team through the Amazonian jungle and rivers to complete a 688-kilometer race just because one of them had given it a meatball during one of the earlier halts.

1011. Although natural gas only became commonly used in the 1800s, the Han Dynasty of China drilled for natural gas, transported it in pipelines and gas containers and burned it on stoves as far back as 200 BC.

1012. There are so many castles in France that some are up for sale cheaper than two-bedroom apartments in big cities like New York City and Sydney.

1013. Bearded vultures wear makeup. They like to alter their appearance by rubbing their necks and heads in iron-rich soil to change their white feathers to a bright reddish-orange. The older and more socially dominant birds wear the most makeup to show off and appear more intimidating.

1014. A lot of old movie theaters used to have something called cry rooms where you could literally take your children if they were becoming disruptive. This way you could still enjoy the movie while not disturbing the other movie goers.

1015. There's a spray that makes everything smell like a cat's head. Cat owners have been known to compare their cat's head to the smell of sunshine or freshly baked bread. A company in Japan spent four months sniffing cats to bottle the scent.

1016. It would take you 10 years to view all of the photos that were shared on Snapchat in the last hour alone.

1017. A group called the Manike Club in Japan created zoo jeans to raise money for the World Wildlife Fund and the local Kamine zoo in Hitoshi city. Lions, tigers, and bears designed the genes by tearing into them and creating distressed jeans. The jeans are then auctioned off for charity.

1018. There's a competition called the World's Biggest Liar held annually in England. Competitors from around the world are given five minutes to tell the biggest and most convincing lie they can think of. Believe it or not politicians and lawyers are banned from entering the competition because they're thought to be too good at lying.

1019. The Burj Al Arab in Dubai is the only seven star hotel in the entire world. However the hotel's management never uses this term to describe itself. The notion was brought about by a British journalist who described the Burj Al Arab as "above and beyond anything she had ever seen" and called it a seven star hotel.

1020. Roger Frisch, a concert violinist was awake when he had brain surgery to get rid of his tremors. His surgeons got a private concert during the surgery as Frisch played the violin while the doctors worked on his brain.

1021. A 17 year old refugee named Aslan Al Hakim refused to leave his puppy Rose in Syria during the refugee crisis, and carried her more than 300 miles to safety.

1022. A grandmother in Vicenza, Italy accidentally sent two adults and three children to the hospital when she made them cocoa with packets that expired back in 1990.

1023. In Japan eating Christmas dinner at KFC is so popular that two hour lines form at some locations waiting for people to get in.

1024. In the Philippines there's banana ketchup. During World War II there was actually a shortage of tomatoes, so they had to use bananas as a replacement to replace ketchup. It's made from mashed bananas, sugar, vinegar, and spices.

1025. In rich countries, obesity is more common among the less educated, but in poor countries obesity is common among the highly educated.

1026. Confidential data from the maritime industry that leaked revealed that one giant container ship can emit the same amount of cancer and asthma-causing chemicals as 50 million cars. That is while the top 15 largest container ships together in the world may be emitting as much pollution as all 760 million cars on earth.

1027. The human heart has three types of blood vessels; arteries, veins and capillaries. Arteries carry oxygenated blood away from the heart. Capillaries connect them to the veins, and veins return the used blood back to the heart.

1028. 7% of the population triggers a sneeze reflex when they stare at a bright light such as the sun or a strong light bulb and of that 7%, 94% of those people are Caucasian.

1029. Simo Hayha, the deadliest sniper in World War II, with over 505 confirmed kills, never once used a telescopic sight.

1030. Sturre Bergwall was known in the 90s as a notorious killer in Sweden. He confessed to over 30 murders and other crimes. But, as it turns out, he was actually just a compulsive and manipulative liar and he never once killed a person or did a crime.

1031. La petite Syrah, a wine bar and bistro in Nice, France, charges extra for rude customers. People who just ask for coffee have to pay €7.50 while adding a please drops the price to €4.25. And if you say "hello, a coffee please." Then you only have to pay €1.40.

1032. In the 1960's and 70's, professional bowlers were international celebrities who made twice as much money as NFL stars at the time.

1033. It's believed that the term sandwich was named after John Montagu, fourth Earl of Sandwich, a town in the county of Kent in southeast England. He would ask his servants to bring him slices of meat between two slices of bread while he was gambling at a table so that he wouldn't have to leave the game.

1034. President Reagan saved Harley Davidson Motorcycles by raising tariffs 45% on Japanese bikes that entered the country.

1035. According to a study published in the proceedings of the National Academy of Sciences, female named storms have historically killed more people because people neither consider them as risky, nor take the same precautions as the male named storms.

1036. In 2008, a Jamaican beach called "Coral Spring Beach" was actually stolen and the thieves were never caught. They achieved this by stealing massive amounts of sand until it basically wasn't a beach any more.

1037. We not only have fingerprints, but also toe prints that have been used in criminal cases.

1038. The headphone jack on your smartphone has remained relatively unchanged other than size since 1878.

1039. Rats are a delicacy in Thailand.

1040. The Taj Mahal in India took over 22 years to build. Construction began in 1632 and finished in 1653. It was built when Emperor Shah Jahan was filled with grief over his passing wife and wanted to create a testament to their love.

1041. Our mouths secrete approximately one liter of saliva per day.
1042. Reykjavik in Iceland actually heat their sidewalks and streets to keep them free of ice and snow. Since they began installing these heated roads over a decade ago, they've enjoyed significant savings from not having to spend taxpayer money on snow removal services.
1043. Bald eagles build nests that are typically around five feet (1.5 meters) in diameter. They often use the same nests year after year and they could become even bigger, as big as nine feet and weighing as much as two tons.
1044. The Chinese soft shell turtle is the first animal known to be able to pee out of its mouth. This was first discovered by researchers at the National University of Singapore, who noticed that turtles would stick their heads into puddles of water and wiggle their tongues, but they weren't drinking.
1045. A group of hippos is called a crash.
1046. In Venezuela, a liter of water costs more than a liter of fuel. Even with the sudden price hikes in 2016 of 1,329% for 91 octane-related gasoline and over 6,000% for 95 octane, gasoline still remains cheaper than clean drinking water.
1047. At one point after its launch, Kim Kardashian's emoji app was making $1,000,000 a minute.
1048. An American teenager named Ethan Couch, who killed four pedestrians while driving drunk, was given no prison time after claiming Affluenza, a mental illness for being too wealthy.
1049. In 2015, Russia opened a military Disneyland called Patriot Park where visitors, including children, can ride in tanks, shoot guns and buy and sell military gear.
1050. Luna moth doesn't have a mouth so it doesn't eat. It only lives for about one week and its sole purpose is to mate.
1051. Alexander Solonick was a Russian hitman known as super killer, famous for killing around 30 mob bosses before becoming one himself. Ironically he was strangled to death just two years later after he started his own criminal organization.

1052. The Kids Wish Network was named the worst charity in the United States in 2013. According to a report only 3 cents out of every dollar raised actually went to granting the wishes of children while the rest of the money went directly into the pockets of the charity organizations operators.

1053. In 2001, the uncle of a boy named Jessie Arbogast, wrestled a 7-foot bull shark to retrieve the severed arm of his nephew. After saving Jesse, the uncle dived back in, seized the shark, and wrestled it to shore, where a ranger shot it. The arm was pried from its gullet, put on ice, rushed to the hospital, and unbelievably successfully sewed back on.

1054. Neil Harbisson is the world's first cyborg artist. He has an antenna implanted in his skull that allows him to hear colors and see sounds, and he can also connect to nearby devices such as bluetooth and the internet.

1055. The reason that buildings in Hong Kong have gaping holes in them is to allow dragons free passage from their mountain homes to the sea.

1056. In the Godfather film, McCluskey's shooting was done by building a fake forehead on top of actor Sterling Hayden. A gap was cut in the middle, filled with fake blood, and bunged up with prosthetic flesh. The plug was then yanked out with a fishing line to make a hole suddenly appear.

1057. According to the patent for toilet paper, the creator, Seth Wheeler, made a drawing that officially shows that toilet paper should go over, not under.

1058. A woman once took part in a search for a missing tourist in Iceland only to realize hours later that she was indeed, the missing person.

1059. A Russian suicide bomber with the intent of killing hundreds in Moscow on New Year's Eve of 2015 had her plan foiled when her wireless carrier sent her a text message wishing her a Happy New Year which triggered her belt bomb killing her, and her alone.

1060. If somebody reports their company for tax evasion in the United States, he or she will receive 15 to 30% of the amount collected. One person named Bradley C. Birkenfeld was a whistleblower on the USB AG Swiss Bank tax evasion scheme and received $104 million as a reward.

1061. In 2013, a man in Michigan whose house was set to be demolished, switched his house numbers with his neighbor, and the crew ended up demolishing the wrong house.

1062. It's possible to die from drowning up to 24 hours after leaving water. It's known as dry drowning where victims can be walking and talking while their lungs are actually filled with water.

1063. Chinchilla fur is so thick and soft that fleas will suffocate if they try to live in it.

1064. The Pigg-O-Stat is a device that has been around since the 1960s where radiologists can safely immobilize babies and young children who can't sit still during an x-ray.

1065. Researchers from the University of Queensland and the University of New South Wales have found that people with dark eyes are more agreeable, while people with blue eyes tend to be more competitive.

1066. There is an unnamed species of octopus that currently exist that scientists think are so cute that they're actually pushing to have it named "Opisthoteuthis Adorabilis."

1067. Antarctica contains 90% of all the ice on the planet in an area that's just under one and a half times the size of the United States. The amount of ice there is staggering. In some parts, such as east Antarctica, ice averages 1.2 miles (1.9 kilometers) thick, but despite its thick ice, Antarctica is classified as a desert because so little moisture falls from the sky every year.

1068. According to scientists at Los Alamos National Laboratory's Lujan Neutron Scattering Center, the world's largest gold crystal was found years ago in Venezuela. It's the size of a golf ball and weighs half a pound and is estimated to be worth $1.5 million.

1069. There's a new dining craze known as 'Dinner in the Sky' available in 15 countries around the world where you actually eat your food in a racing chair suspended 60 meters above ground.

1070. McDonald's opened their first ski-through fast food restaurant in 1996 located in Sweden. You can actually ski up to the counter, order your food, and ski off. They call it 'McSki'.

1071. Peter Mayhew, the actor who played Chewbacca in Star Wars actually had to be accompanied by crew members dressed in brightly colored vests while filming in the forest of the Pacific Northwest. This was to ensure that he wasn't shot by hunters who would mistake him for Bigfoot.

1072. The Center for Retail Research in Britain found that the most stolen food item in the world is cheese. In fact, 4% of all cheese sold was actually stolen.

1073. There are actually miniature guide horses that the blind can use as an alternative to seeing-eye-dogs. They have several perceived advantages to that of a dog, including the average lifespan of 30 years and having 350-degree vision.

1074. In 1967, during the Nigerian Civil War, both sides agreed to a 48-hour ceasefire because Pele was in town to play an exhibition soccer game and everyone wanted to be free to watch it without having to worry about the war.

1075. London has a cereal cafe known as 'The Cereal Killer Café' where you can eat hundreds of different kinds of cereal from around the world.

1076. The Lion King was originally called "The King of the Jungle." That is until the Disney team learned that lions don't live in a jungle.

1077. There are special bins in Mexico City where you can put your dog poo in it and in exchange you get free wifi, and in fact the more poo the longer the free wifi.

1078. Coca-Cola has made over 3,500 different kinds of beverages. That means that if you drink one per day it would take over nine years for you to try them all.

1079. Fennec foxes mate for life. The male fox has become especially aggressive towards each other when mating season approaches in order to protect their mates.

1080. Russian billionaire Vasily Klyukin wanted hospitals to be more welcoming, so he designed one to resemble a luxury yacht called White Sails Hospital, that a Tunisian businessman plans to build over the next 15 years.

1081. There is a normal barbie called The Lammily Doll where the doll has brunette hair, cellulite, stretch marks, freckles, acne and more. She was also given the proportions of a typical 19 year old.

1082. When Gary Knell the president and CEO of the Sesame Street workshop was asked whether Bert and Ernie were gay he responded that they're not gay, they're not straight, they're puppets, they don't exist below the waist.

1083. Elvis Presley only failed one class at school. That was music class.

1084. Towards the later years in his life Voltaire developed a habit of living near country borders so that he could escape by crossing the border if his writing angered the authorities.

1085. After hurricane Katrina, the Amir of Gatar donated 100 million dollars to help rebuild housing, hospitals, and schools. He visited the area a few years later after the disaster to check on its progress.

1086. There is a 70 meter long organ on the coast of Zadar, Croatia. The organ, designed by architect Nikola Basic has 35 tubes that make music whenever waves crash into them.

1087. The last individual of a single species is called an endling. When it dies the species is extinct.

1088. Tiny pseudoscorpions which are usually about 2 to 8 millimeters long are often found in rooms with dusty books. They actually protect the books by feeding on booklice and dust mites.

1089. In 2014 a homeowner in England accidentally left a spare bedroom window open for three months. This allowed about 5000 wasps to sneak through and build a massive nest on the bed. Disturbingly, the wasps chewed through about 20 centimeters worth of mattress and pillows but pest control managed to at least salvage the crochet blanket in the house.

1090. Despite their size difference, praying mantises can easily catch and eat hummingbirds.

1091. White coke is a clear colored coca-cola commissioned by Soviet marshal Gregory Zhukov in the 1940s. He requested it because he was a fan of coke, but didn't want to be seen drinking it in public, so we asked for a color to resemble vodka instead.

1092. In 1992, the CEO's of Southwest Airlines and Steven's Aviation settled the dispute over who would get to use the slogan "Plane Smart" by arm-wrestling instead of dealing with a long drawn-out legal battle.

1093. Babies are actually capable of giving a thumbs up in the womb.

1094. The Khum Bak river resort in Sri Lanka is a hotel that's shaped like a giant elephant.

1095. When he was only 13 years old, Ashton Kutcher thought about committing suicide, so that he could donate his heart to his brother, who desperately needed a heart transplant for his cardiomyopathy.

1096. The pink fairy armadillo is the smallest species of armadillo. It is a mere four inches long and weighs about a hundred grams.

1097. In Las Vegas, an average of five to seven adults are reported missing every day and more than 200 a month.

1098. 40 to 50 million years ago, Antarctica's climate was very similar to modern day California's.

1099. If you leave towels, chairs, or sun umbrellas overnight to save a spot on busy Italian beaches, officials will take what you left behind and fine you about $220 to get your property back.

1100. The very last McDonald's hamburger and fries in Iceland is on display at a bus hostel in Reykjavik right now. You can even watch real-time footage of it over a live stream. A man purchased it back in October 30th of 2009, and it's still on display.

1101. In South Korea, if you win gold at the Asian Games or any medal at the Olympics, you are exempt from the country's military service, which is mandatory for able-bodied males.

1102. The walnut-sized male blanket octopus tears off the tentacles of passing Portuguese man o' war jellyfish as a defense mechanism.

1103. Tigers have a retinal adaptation that reflects light back to the retina, which makes their night vision six times better than humans'.

1104. According to the Death Penalty Information Center, since 1973, 156 people have been exonerated and freed from death row.

1105. There is a Switzerland-based company that for the cost of $29,000 will name your baby for you.

1106. Kamikaze or exploding ants from Southeast Asia kill themselves when under threat. They have a toxic substance in their heads and in two large glands on the sides of their bodies that are filled with poison. Under threat they literally explode their heads or rupture their bodies to spray the poison to cover the predator.

1107. In medieval times, bras were called breast bags.

1108. The 2016 Olympics in Rio was the first time in Olympic history that South American country had hosted the games.

1109. The phrase always a bridesmaid, never a bride was popularized by Listerine in ads featuring a lovelorn woman unable to find a husband due to her halitosis. The same ad coined the term halitosis.

1110. According to an analysis done by Swift Key, Canada uses the poop emoji more than any other country. Hearts are number one in France, even beating the standard smiley and Australia leads the world in alcohol and drug related emojis.

1111. The original creator for the Barbie Doll, Jack Ryan, had previously designed military grade missiles.

1112. In January of 2016, McDonald's Japan introduced for a limited time French-fries drizzled with two kinds of chocolate sauce.

1113. United States once attempted to buy Greenland in 1946 for 100 million dollars.

1114. A person who sleeps too much, sits too much, and isn't active enough, is more than four times as likely to die early.

1115. In 2012, a woman named Rebekah Speight, of Dakota City, successfully sold a Chicken McNugget on ebay for, 8100 dollars because it simply looked like George Washington.

1116. Ukrainian engineer, Vladimir Tatarenko, has designed an airplane with a detachable cabin. In the event of an emergency, the cabin breaks off, deploys parachutes, and floats passengers safely to sea or ground.

1117. Tim Hawking added swear words to his dad, Stephen Hawking's, voice synthesizer as a prank.

1118. Following Marilyn Monroe's death, Joe DiMaggio was so devastated that he held a private funeral barring all of Hollywood's elite, delivering roses to her grave three times a week for over 20 years. He never remarried, and his final words were I'll finally get to see Marilyn.

1119. In order to protect the city's water, the Los Angeles department of water and power purchased 80 million hollow black balls to cover its reservoirs to stop the sunlight from triggering dangerous chemical reactions.

1120. After losing a battle in world war two because of taking a tea break, the British army perfected the art of brewing tea inside of a tank by creating the British army boiling vessel. A built-in kettle for armored vehicles.

1121. It is illegal to die in London's Houses of parliament.

1122. Pteridophobia is the fear of ferns.

1123. Dog blood type is different than the types found in people. In fact, there are six major blood types, but amazingly, 42% of dogs have the same type, which is universal.

1124. According to National Geographic explorer Zeb Hogan, the wels catfish is the largest freshwater fish in Europe. It can grow up to 15 feet long, weigh as much as 660 pounds, and live for decades, possibly as long as 80 years.

1125. Sweat is actually odorless. It's only when bacteria on the skin and hair metabolize the proteins and fatty acids in sweat that it produces an unpleasant scent.

1126. Baby blue whales can consume up to 150 gallons of its mother's milk a day.

1127. The word dude was first used in the 1800s as an insult towards young men who were too concerned with keeping up with the latest fashions.

1128. John Cena, WWE superstar, has granted more than 400 Make-A-Wish requests, more than anyone else in the charity's history.

1129. Mathematician Paul Erdos could calculate in his head, given a person's age, how many seconds that they had lived, when he was four.

1130. According to his brother, Vincent Van Gogh's last words were, "The sadness will last forever."

1131. Believe it or not, coloring books for grownups are a huge trend, and publishers actually struggle to keep up with demand. The books are used successfully to reduce stress, relieve anxiety and as rehabilitation aids for patients that are recovering from strokes.

1132. Sam Griner from the 'Successful Kid' memes used his success to start a GoFundMe page, which raised nearly $100,000 for his dad's kidney transplant.

1133. There is a town in Arizona called nothing and it's a ghost town. So quite literally nothing is there.

1134. Bob Marley's song No Woman, No Cry is actually No woman, Nuh cry in Jamaica. This actually translates to no woman, don't cry and the song is about growing up in the ghetto and persuading a woman that things will get better so don't cry.

1135. Istanbul has an estimated 150,000 stray dogs. A company called huge din has created a vending machine where food and water for the dogs can be dispensed when people recycle the plastic bottles.

1136. Guide dogs are able to go against their owners instructions when they think their order is unsafe. This is called intelligent disobedience.

1137. Underwater hockey is a sport where two teams compete to push a puck across the bottom of a swimming pool into the opposing team's goal. It originated in England in 1954 and is also called Octopush.

1138. There's a tradition in Glasgow of placing a traffic cone on the head of the Duke of Wellington Statue. The cost of removing the traffic cone costs an estimated 10,000 pounds a year.

1139. It's illegal not to flush the toilet in Singapore. For failing to flush, you will be fined $150 and police officers have been known to check.

1140. Buzz Aldrin's maiden name was, coincidentally, Moon.

1141. Just one percent of friendships formed in the 7th grade are still intact by the 12th grade, according to a study by Psychological Science.

1142. Architects in Iceland wanted to push the appearance of utility towers beyond their basic functional structures. So, they created a design proposal called "The Land of Giants." Essentially, it turns electrical pylons into human-shaped sculptures.

1143. Portuguese artist David Oliveira uses wire to draw in the air by creating sculptures that look like pencil sketches.

1144. There is a prison in Finland where the only thing keeping inmates in is a yellow picket fence.

1145. 'Anhedonia' is the word for a feeling when you cannot find joy in things that usually bring you joy.

1146. In 2001, Pizza Hut paid the Russian space agency to send a pizza to the International Space Station at a cost of one million dollars.

1147. 20-year-old Kiran Cable from South Wales was with his girlfriend so much that his friends say that he actually disappeared from their lives so much so that after 18 months of unreturned calls and emails. Fifty of Cable's friends decided to surprise him with a mock funeral that included a coffin, a hearse, and even a eulogy.

1148. In the 1970s Senator Larry Pressler refused to take a bribe that was offered from the FBI. He was called a Hero for doing so but he didn't think turning down a bribe should be considered heroic.

1149. You are most likely to come up with a great idea when doing monotonous tasks such as exercising driving or showering. This is because we are the most relaxed and least distracted so dopamine is flowing through our bodies and triggering our thoughts.

1150. The Great Gatsby originally sold very poorly with only 20,000 copies sold in the first year it was published. F.Scott Fitzgerald died believing that his work was a failure.

1151. It isn't entirely true that no two snowflakes are alike. Snowflakes actually fall in only one of 35 different shapes.

1152. By the end of your life, odds are you will have spent over 20,000 minutes kissing. That's literally two weeks of your life with your lips locked with someone else's.

1153. Dolphins are the only other species that are documented to have sex just for pleasure and not just for procreation.

1154. There are only four words in the English language that end with -dous. They are tremendous, horrendous, stupendous, and hazardous.

1155. A tiger's stripes are on their skin, not just their fur. More collect phone calls are made on Father's Day than any other day of the year. AT&T reported on average, 83 million calls were made on Father's Day, compared to 106 million on Mother's Day, but 27% more Father's Day calls were collect.

1156. Pearls will actually dissolve when immersed in vinegar. A pearl is mostly calcium carbonate, which is susceptible to even the weakest acid solution.

1157. On March 3rd, 1934, gangster John Dillinger escaped from a jail in Indiana with the help of a wooden gun that was smuggled in to him by one of his attorneys.

1158. The first technical casualty of the Civil War was killed during a 100-gun salute. A cannon prematurely discharged and killed Private Daniel Hough of the First U.S. Artillery.

1159. McDonald's in the Netherlands has a place mat called a McTrax where you can make music while you eat. To make it work, you place your phone on the mat, get an app, and then compose your music including your voice.

1160. According to the Guinness World Records, the United States holds the record for the most medals won at a single summer Olympic games. At the 1904 Olympics, held in St. Louis, Missouri, they won 78 gold medals, 82 silver, and 79 bronze for a total of 239.

1161. Edgar Allen Poe once published a novel where a ship crew becomes stranded with no food and one member named Richard Parker is sacrificed for food. Disturbingly 45 years later in 1884 a yacht sank on route from England to Australia. The four men crew didn't have enough food to survive and one boy was killed by the other three for food. His name was Richard Parker.

1162. Despite having DNA evidence of the suspect, German police could not prosecute a 6.8 million dollar jewel heist because the DNA belonged to identical twins and there was no evidence to prove which one of them was actually the culprit.

1163. Bruises turn colors because your body is breaking down and reabsorbing the hemoglobin that leaked from the broken blood vessels in your body.

1164. At full sprint a cheetah spends more time flying than in contact with the ground.

1165. Hundreds of prisoners were left to die in their cells during Hurricane Katrina as officials abandoned Orleans Parish Prison.

1166. Elephants are more intelligent than you think. One elephant in India was trained to place logs in pre dug holes for a ceremony. On one occasion it refused to place a log in a hole where a dog was sleeping and waited until the dog was chased away to lower the post into the hole.

1167. In 2007, a Doberman Pinscher (a dog breed) named Khan actually saved a baby girl from a deadly king brown snake attack by grabbing the girl by the diaper and flinging her to safety and taking a venomous bite to the paw in her place.

1168. In 1809, the Spanish town of Huescar declared war on Denmark then forgot about it for 172 years. Not a single shot was fired, and no one was killed, and a peace treaty was finally signed in 1981 when a historian found the official declaration and realized that they were actually supposed to be fighting.

1169. There's a popular variation of 'Yo Momma' type jokes in Kenya that goes a little something like this. "Your family is so stupid you gave your chickens hot water so they can lay boiled eggs."

1170. Google Chrome's dinosaur Wifi error message is actually also a game. So, next time you're angry at your internet for breaking, just press the spacebar and you will witness your T-Rex jump. Just don't let him land on the cactus or it'll be game over.

1171. There are playgrounds in England, Finland, Germany, and the US designed specifically for aging residents. They feature low-impact exercise equipment designed to promote balance and flexibility such as elliptical machines, static bikes, and flexors.

1172. Starting on July 19th, 2016, T-Mobile gave all of its customers a year of unlimited data to play Pokémon GO. They also offered 50% off mobile accessories such as portable power packs and more because so many people's phones were dying.

1173. In June of 2016, there was a massive theft of Twitter usernames and passwords involving nearly 33 million customers. According to the security company, LeakedSource, over 120,000 people had used the password one, two, three, four, five, six.

1174. There's a sport called joggling where you jog and juggle at the same time. It was invented by a man named Bill Giduz who would juggle balls on a running track to increase his coordination when he realized that the pace of the three-ball juggling pattern easily matched a wide range of running cadences.

1175. When General Motors unveiled the Camaro name in 1966, Automotive Press asked Chevrolet product managers "What is a Camaro?" And they were told it's a small vicious animal that eats mustangs.

1176. Steve Jobs refused to let his own kids have iPads and limited their use of technology to a minimum.

1177. LSD was first synthesized in 1938, but it wasn't until five years later that its creator, Albert Hofmann, accidentally consumed it discovering its hallucinogenic properties. It was then packaged nine years later for psychiatric uses.

1178. The world's first ligers were born in 2013. A white lion and a tiger had four male cubs which are now the rarest big cats on earth.

1179. After American physicist Richard Feynman was named the world's smartest man by Omni Magazine, his mother was actually quoted as saying, "If that's the world's smartest man, God help us."

1180. In the entire Lord of the Rings trilogy, no two female characters ever speak to each other.

1181. In the late 1900s, Howard Hughes bought an entire casino named Silver Slipper just so that he could tear down their neon sign. This is because it was visible from Hughes' bedroom, and apparently it was keeping him up at night.

1182. Tom Monaghan, founder of Domino's Pizza met his wife on his first pizza delivery back in 1962.

1183. Violet Jessop was a ship nurse on the Britannic, the Olympic and the Titanic. While on board the Olympic, it collided with a warship and nearly sank. While on the Titanic, it hit an iceberg and sank, and the Britannic hit an underwater mine and sank, yet Violet survived all three.

1184. Justo Gallego Martinez, a 90 year old former monk, has been building an unauthorized cathedral in Spain since 1961. He mostly works alone for 10 hours a day, 6 days a week.

1185. The earth's day-night cycle is growing longer year by year. And 620,000,000 million years ago, an earth day was only 21.9 hours.

1186. During the cold winters, the Alaskan wood frog becomes a frog shaped block of ice. It literally stops breathing and its heart stops beating. Then, when spring arrives, the frog thaws and returns to normal, and goes along its merry way.

1187. More salt is used for deicing roads with 8% of global manufactured salt going there compared to 6% for human consumption.

1188. Every time that you recall an event, your brain distorts it just a little bit. Basically when you remember something that happened in the past, you're actually just remembering the last time that you remembered it, and so on.

1189. 18-year-old, Andrej Ciesielski, was arrested for climbing the Great Pyramid of Giza and taking photos, after which he shared with his thousands of followers, who loved watching him travel the world just to climb stuff.

1190. There's a class of people in Japan referred to as cyber-homeless, who live at cyber cafes, because they're actually a cheaper alternative to an apartment. The cafes offer free showers and even sell underwear.

1191. A Chinese man bought and raised two puppies, cared for them despite their frequent killing and eating of chickens and discovered later that they were bears.

1192. Blowing smoke up your ass actually used to be a common cure for many ailments.

1193. Japan has a network of roads that actually plays music as you drive over them at the correct speed.

1194. A South Korean man named Woo Bum-kon committed a mass murder because he was enraged from being woken by his girlfriend trying to swat a fly on his chest.

1195. Yokohama Japan has an annual festival devoted entirely to Pikachu. The Pikachu outbreak is a week-long festival where masses of dancing Pikachus, along with countless statues, completely take over the city.

1196. Mike Tyson first snorted cocaine when he was just 11 years old, and was given alcohol when he was just an infant.

1197. George R.R. Martin was so impressed with Jack Gleeson's portrayal of Joffrey in 'Game of Thrones' that he sent him a personal letter saying congratulations on your marvelous performance, everyone hates you.

1198. Arch West, the inventor of Doritos was buried with Doritos sprinkled over his body.

1199. In 2014 a man named Chistian Poincheval invented a range of pills aimed at making people's farts smell like either chocolate or roses.

1200. One of the biggest reasons why night vision goggles are green is because the human eye is the most sensitive to light wavelengths near 555 nanometers aka green and can differentiate between more shades of this green than any other color.

1201. In 1923 Bobby the wonder dog tracked 2500 miles (4100 kilometers) across the United States to reunite with his owners after he got lost in Indian during a family road trip.

1202. Property owners in New York City can actually request to have trees planted on their street for free. They're even allowed to suggest what species to plant.

1203. In Japan, there's a condition called Hikikomori where around a million people, mostly men, have locked themselves in their bedrooms for years creating social and health problems.

1204. There's a replica of Noah's Ark in Williamstown, Kentucky. It was built by creationist ministry. It is exactly the dimensions specified in the book of Genesis at 450 feet long, 67 feet high, and 46 feet wide and cost about $100 million to make.

1205. The Antarctic Polar Desert is the largest desert on Earth. It covers the continent of Antarctica and is the size of about 5.5 million square miles (8.8 million square kilometers).

1206. The world's most expensive aquarium fish is the Asian Arowana, also known as the dragon fish. It's believed by the Chinese to bring good luck and prosperity due to its red color and coin-like scales. This fish has sold for up to $300,000.

1207. Siberia has a population density of less than eight people per one square mile. This is extra shocking considering that Siberia covers 77% of all of Russia and has an area of more than 50 times that of the U.K., but, yet, has half the population.

1208. During the American Civil War, if you were drafted, you could actually pay someone $300 to go in your place. This was called commutation and was intended to raise money for the war effort, but was often heavily criticized that it was better at raising money than troops.

1209. China invented fireworks, but Italy gave them their colors. Colors are created using metallic powders. Calcium makes orange.

Sodium makes yellow, and Barium makes green. Also, cylindrical tubes create whistling sounds. Aluminum flakes make hissing noises, and flash powder makes loud boom sounds.

1210. According to a study done by National Geographic, the same gene that gives humans the urge to travel is also responsible for ADHD and thrill-seeking behavior.

1211. The reason that paper cuts hurt so much is that the cut often bleeds very little or not at all leaving the skin's pain receptors open to air.

1212. A man named Chen Si spends every weekend of his life at the Nanjing Yangtze River Bridge which is the world's number one suicide bridge. He does it to save people from jumping, and in fact, he has saved 144 people from killing themselves.

1213. ISIS has so much money that it's wealthier than several actual countries. The group makes about $1 million to $5 million a day.

1214. There's an annual photo contest called "The Comedy Wildlife Photography Awards." Entries consist of the funniest animal wildlife pictures that photographers accidentally or intentionally captured throughout their career.

1215. Boeing has created a new metal called "microlattice" that's 99.99% air. So light in fact that the metal can sit on top of a dandelion without crushing it.

1216. When he died in 1937, John D. Rockefeller's estate equaled 1.5% of America's total economic output. To put that into perspective for you, today that's the equivalent of four times the amount of Bill Gates net worth when it was at its peak.

1217. Saltwater Brewery, from Florida, has partnered up with the ad agency, We Believers, to create fully edible six-pack beer can packaging. It's made from byproducts of the brewing process like wheat and barley, and is fully biodegradable and completely digestible. They are just as strong as the plastic ones, but if an animal or bird gets caught in one, they can actually snack on it and quickly decompose it.

1218. Cobwebs actually have antifungal and antiseptic properties that keep bacteria away, minimizing the chance of infection. In fact, in ancient times, the Greeks and Romans would use cobwebs to treat cuts. Soldiers also used spider webs to heal wounds. They would combine honey and vinegar to clean the wounds and then cover it with balled-up spider webs.

1219. The female Burmese Python is able to incubate her eggs by raising her body temperature by as much as seven degrees warmer than air temperature. They accomplish this by frequently hiccupping or having muscle spasms.

1220. Ancient Egyptians used to put dead mice into the mouths of people to treat toothaches. They also mashed up dead mouse paste with other ingredients to treat patients with pain.

1221. In 2015, astronomers located a gigantic cloud of methyl alcohol called methanol surrounding a stellar nursery, measuring over 310 billion miles (500 billion km) across. Over time, it could actually help astronomers understand how some of the most massive stars in the universe are formed.

1222. Tibetan nuns can actually change their core body temperatures with a form of meditation called gitumo. Using temperature measurements, a team of researchers recorded the internal temperature of the nuns in the freezing cold of the Himalayas. The nuns were able to increase their core body temperature up to almost 101 degrees Fahrenheit (38 degrees celsius).

1223. Researchers at Murdoch University in Perth have discovered goldfish as long as 12 inches and weighing as much as 4.2 pounds (1.9 kg) in the Bath River in the southwest of Western Australia. They think it's the result of people releasing their goldfish into the water. This is because in the wild, that's how big they can grow.

1224. According to the National Oceanic and Atmospheric Administration and NASA, July 2016 was the hottest month in 136 years of record keeping.

1225. Dyslexics see numbers and letters backwards. It's a reading disorder, not a vision or seeing disorder, which means that Braille readers can also be dyslexic.

1226. According to a study published in the Journal of Behavior Therapy and Experimental Psychiatry, mood can affect how we walk and vice versa. We walk slumped-shoulderd if we're sad, bouncing if we're happy. Making people imitate a happy walk actually made them feel happier, and sadder if they were imitating a sad way of walking.

1227. Queen Elizabeth and her husband, Prince Philip, are third cousins.

1228. According to Guinness World Records, the oldest tree known to have been planted by humans is 2,300 years old. The sacred fig, or Bow Tree was planted in Sri Lanka in 288 BC.

1229. In India as well as other parts of the world, standing babas are people who have taken a vow to never sit, lay, or squat for 12 years in order to transport their psyches into a realm of spiritual awareness not experienced by sitters. They stand before a small hammock in which to rest their arms during the day and torso at night. One leg must be on the ground at all times.

1230. Most mammals don't live long past their reproductive years. Only a few that we know do, such as the killer whales, pilot whales, and possibly some great apes and human beings.

1231. The national sport of Afghanistan is called Buzkashi where a headless carcass of a calf or goat is kept in the center of a field and two opposing teams, on horseback, try to get hold of the carcass and carry it to the goal area. The game can sometimes last for days.

1232. In the small town of El Valle de Anton, Panama, there are trees growing that have square trunks. It's believed that this strange anomaly of nature doesn't occur anywhere else in the world. In fact, experts from the University of Florida, took a few tree seedlings to see if they will retain their rectangular shape if planted elsewhere in the world, and they didn't when planted in other locations.

1233. In 1818, when Abraham Lincoln was nine, his mother, Nancy, died of a mysterious milk sickness that was sweeping across southern Indiana. It turned out the strange disease was due to drinking tainted milk from a cow that had ingested poisonous white snakeroot.

1234. Mary, Queen of Scots, became queen at only six days old. This is because her father died and she was his successor.

1235. During its lifetime, an oyster changes its sex from male to female and back several times.

1236. During his entire life, artist Vincent Van Gogh sold exactly one painting, "Red Vineyard at Arles".

1237. The spider, Calponia harrisonfordi, was named for the star of "Raiders of the Lost Ark" and "Star Wars", as a thanks to Harrison Ford who narrated a documentary for the London Museum of Natural History in 1994. The spider itself was discovered in 1993 and is very tiny, only around five millimeters in length, and lives in California.

1238. The only member of the band, Z Z Top, without a beard has the last name, Beard.

1239. Toto from the "Wizard of Oz" was paid $125 a week. This was more than the Munchkin actors were paid.

1240. The fastest healing part on the human body is the tongue. This is due to the rich supply of blood that the tongue receives, making it able to heal twice as fast than any other part of the body.

1241. Montpelier, Vermont is the only state capital without a McDonald's.

1242. Snakes and lizards flick their tongues in the air to capture scent particles. In other words, they smell with their tongues.

1243. The aquarium at the Golden Nugget in Las Vegas has a waterslide also called the Shark Chute where you can go through the tank and see the sharks.

1244. In 2001 Robin Williams met and became friends with Koko the gorilla who communicates in sign language. After hearing about Robin William's death in 2014, Koko signs the word cry and became somber for the rest of the day.

1245. In 2005, a girl in Ethiopia was kidnapped and was saved by three wild lions. The lions unbelievably chased off her kidnappers and stayed with her until the police found her.

1246. In 2015 in Colorado, a mysterious teenager was regularly breaking into homes, stealing snacks, specifically Hot Pockets, and watching people's Netflix. He literally steals no cash or valuables, only snacks and Netflix.

1247. The sun is the most perfect sphere ever observed in nature according to University of Hawaii.

1248. Polish teenager Iga Jasica unexpectedly woke up in the middle of her brain surgery and calmly asked the doctor, "How's it going?" Amazingly she wasn't in any pain so they talked about cats until the surgery was over.

1249. In 2003 two men stole a Boeing 727 from an Angolan airport and were never seen again.

1250. Saudi Arabia is the largest country in the world without a river.

1251. Disney put 500 stormtroopers on the Great Wall of China to promote Star Wars The Force Awakens.

1252. The Soviets found that sniper duties actually fit women the best since snipers are patient, careful, deliberate, can avoid hand to hand combat, and need higher levels of aerobic conditioning than other troops.

1253. The Dai-Ichi Yochien preschool in Japan has a courtyard that collects rainwater into a giant clean puddle that kids can stomp and splash around in.

1254. There is a rare brain disorder called Foreign Accent Syndrome that causes people to involuntarily speak in foreign accents.

1255. Adopting children is actually considered taboo in Korea, and because of this, South Korea's orphans are almost never adopted unless a foreigner adopts them.

1256. In 2015 a Russian man got drunk with his friends, dropped dead, came back to life in the morgue freezer, and then headed off to drink some more.

1257. Despite their bad reputation, great white sharks have only ever attacked people 280 times between 1876 and 2013 globally, and on top of that, only 77 have ever resulted in a fatality. Just for a little comparison, deer kill nearly 200 people a year in the US alone.

1258. Studies from the University of North Carolina concluded that incredibly beautiful people are actually less likely to be hired for a job if they're being interviewed by someone of the same sex. They're also often very lonely because they're viewed as unapproachable and intimidating, and they're even given less care by doctors when being treated for pain.

1259. There are only two countries in the world whose flags do not contain either red, white, or blue. Jamaica and Mauritania.

1260. A newborn Chinese water deer is so adorably small after birth that you could hold it in one hand, but when it grows up, they can weigh as much as 13 kilograms and sprouts fangs, making them look like a vampire deer.

1261. After mismanagement, the social news site Digg, a company that was once valued at $200 million was sold for a mere $500,000.

1262. A previously crystal-blue hot spring located in Yellowstone National Park is actually turning green as the result of tourists throwing good luck coins into it since 1950. It has since been dubbed Fading Glory.

1263. If you went swimming on the moon, you would be able to walk on the water's surface and jump out of the water like a dolphin catching air above water.

1264. The character of Popeye is actually based on a real-life person named Frank "Rocky" Fiegel. He was a local tough guy in Chester, Illinois, and quite similar to the real Popeye. He had some pretty serious forearms.

1265. Alfred Binet, the original inventor of the IQ test, created the methodology to identify students who needed help. He actually deplored its use as a ranking for unitary and linear intelligence.

1266. Lifeguard Thomas Lopez from South Florida was fired after saving someone from drowning because the man he saved wasn't technically in his assigned lifeguard area.

1267. In 1975, a 17-year-old boy was killed while riding his Moped. He was killed exactly one year after his 17-year-old brother was killed while riding the same Moped in the same intersection by the same taxi with the same driver carrying the same passenger.

1268. A creature called the Prasinohaema skink lives on the island of New Guinea and has green blood, bones and tissue. No other vertebrates are known to have green blood, and it's extremely toxic to humans.

1269. The medical term for your butt crack is the intergluteal cleft, also known as the natal cleft and the vertical gluteal crease.

1270. In 1952, Mr. Potato Head was the first-ever toy advertised on TV. Nearly two million were sold in the first year alone, and Mrs. Potato Head came a year later in 1953.

1271. The ad agency FDB Brazil created a doll for Nivea that is made of UV-sensitive material and turns a painful-looking bright red if left out in the sun. Applying sunscreen to it turns it white again. The doll was made to teach children the importance of wearing sunscreen.

1272. If you have an injury to your hand or fingers and there's nerve damage, your fingers won't wrinkle when submerged in water.

1273. 19-year-old Shayla Wiggins from Riverton, Wyoming, found a dead body floating in a river while playing Pokemon Go. She was trying to find a Pokemon from a natural water resource, but she found something' else.

1274. Elvis Presley had a twin brother who was a stillborn. His name was Jesse Garon.

1275. In 1994, Bill Gates bought Leonardo da Vinci's Codex Leicester notebook for $30.8 million. He did it to not only add to his personal collection, but to also help promote Windows Vista's launch by using a program called Turning the Pages 2.0 that lets people browse through virtual versions of the notebook.

1276. Robert F. Kennedy failed third grade. Smaller than his siblings, Bobby was often considered the runt of the family and he even attended nearly a dozen schools as well.

1277. Governments in Iraq and India have imposed an internet blackout during exams to prevent students from cheating.

1278. You can now hire a self-driving taxi in Singapore. During the testing period, the cars had a driver in the front who could take over the wheel at any time, and a researcher in the back who watches the computers. They're equipped with a detection system that uses lasers to operate like radar and two cameras on the dashboard to scan for obstacles and detect traffic light changes.

1279. Hurricane names are recycled every six years, with the exception of hurricanes that have been so deadly and costly that the future use of its name for a different storm would be insensitive.

1280. A Filipino fisherman found a 75-pound natural pearl and kept it hidden under his bed for 10 years. He discovered it in a giant clam and kept it as a good luck charm. It's 170,000 carats.

1281. According to a new study in the Journal of Hand Therapy, millennials have weaker muscles in their hands from all the texting, snapping, scrolling, and gaming that they do, especially the guys.

1282. There's a social anxiety called parthenophobia where you have an abnormal and persistent fear of young girls.

1283. Vampire bats have a protein in their saliva that acts as an anticoagulant, which keeps their victim's blood flowing while they feed. Researchers have actually been studying it to see if it can help dissolve blood clots and help with stroke victims.

1284. In the 1904 Summer Olympics, gymnast George Eiser won three gold medals, two silver, and a bronze, all while wearing a wooden prosthetic leg.

1285. There used to be a sport called ferret-legging, where a ferret is strapped in a contestant's pants, without underwear. The contestant who can stand the teeth and claws the longest wins.

1286. The ALS Association received 101 million dollars in donations compared to 2.8 million the previous year because of the money raised by people doing the ice bucket challenge.

1287. In the United Kingdom and Ireland, you can purchase cyberbullying insurance. The insurance company, Chub, will pay out as much as $74,600 to help with court costs and relocation fees.

1288. In Shanghai, you can have your credit score lowered for not sending greetings or visiting your elderly parents.

1289. There is a hangover clinic in Sydney, Australia. For a whopping $200, you can get one-hour treatments, which includes a half gallon of hydration drip, oxygen therapy, and vitamins to help you recover from a night of too much alcohol.

1290. The average person yawns about 250,000 times over the course of their life and babies in the womb even do it as early as 12 to 14 weeks.

1291. One of the deadliest earthquakes in history happened in Shaanxi, China, on January 23, 1556, killing an estimated 830,000 people. It was later revealed that the magnitude of the quake was approximately eight to 8.3, which isn't nearly the strongest tremor on record, but the quake struck in the middle of an unfortunately densely populated area with poorly constructed buildings and homes, resulting in horrific death tolls.

1292. Scientists from Psychology Today concluded that if a person's body odor smells good to you it means that their immunity genes are opposite to yours. This allows higher chances for people with opposite immunity genes to mate, resulting in offspring with stronger immune systems.

1293. Just 2% of the entire world's population is naturally blonde.

1294. Nissan uses the number 23 in car racing because the number two translates to 'ni' in Japanese, and the number three translates to 'san', hence 23 translates into Nissan.

1295. Neurologists claim that every time you resist acting on your anger, you're actually rewiring your brain to be a calmer and more loving person.

1296. In 1987, Steve Rothstein bought a lifetime, unlimited first-class American Airlines ticket for $250,000. He flew over 10,000 flights, costing the company $21 million. They terminated his ticket in 2008.

1297. A study conducted at Columbia University concluded that people born in the month of May, may have the lowest risk of illness and disease.

1298. Leonardo da Vinci invented the scissors.
1299. Lizards can self-amputate their tails for protection. And they grow them back after only a few months.
1300. Like fingerprints, everyone's tongue print is different.
1301. Actress Candice Bergen's father left $10,000 to his ventriloquist dummy and zero to her. He said the dummy had been my constant companion from whom I have never been separated, even for a day.
1302. Microwaves use more electricity to power their clocks than they do to heat up your food.
1303. There is something called non visible art where works are imagined by the artists and described to the audience. In 2011 a woman named Amie Davidson bought one of these pieces for $10,000 saying she identified with the ideology of the non visible art project.
1304. There is a 200 foot (61 meter) long pink stuffed bunny on the top of a hill in the Piedmont region of Italy. It's there for Hikers to enjoy and should decay completely by 2025.
1305. Cats have adapted to fall from great heights. When they fall they reach terminal velocity and they twist their bodies so that they can position their feet under their bodies to land themselves.
1306. In 2012 a man named Seth Horvitz ordered a TV from amazon and instead got a military grade assault rifle instead.
1307. The walled City in St-Malo France is notorious for being a safe haven for pirates.
1308. A study done in 2010 shows that women find men in red to be more attractive. The color makes men appear more powerful and higher in status which leads to the attraction.
1309. Martha Stewart once dated Anthony Hopkins, but broke up with him after seeing "Silence of the Lambs". She stated that she was unable to avoid associating Hopkins with the character of Hannibal Lecter.
1310. Japan was invaded by the strong Mongol army twice, and both times were saved by the harsh storms that crippled the Mongols. They called these storms "kamikaze" or divine winds.

1311. Zach Braff punched a 12-year-old for spraying fake paint on his Porsche as part of a prank on the show "Punk'd."

1312. During the Afghanistan War, when his team was ambushed, outnumbered, and under fire, British Corporal Sean Jones ordered his men to affix bayonets to their guns and charge across 80 meters of open ground against the Taliban forces. And unbelievably, it worked. Enemy forces scattered, fleeing the fight, due to the unexpected move.

1313. Spain cheated in the 2000 Summer Paralympics. 10 out of the 12 players on their roster were encouraged to pretend that they were mentally disabled, and they actually had no mental disability.

1314. Canada consumes the most donuts and has the most donut shops per capita of any country in the world.

1315. Jack Nicholson grew up believing that his mother was his sister and his grandparents were his parents. He didn't find out the truth until both his mother and grandmother had died.

1316. It's possible for stem cells to extend human life. In 2014 researchers in Pittsburgh injected white mice with stem cells. Now normally their usual lifespan is 21 days but after injection they lived for an extra 71 days. This is the equivalent of an 80 year old human being living to be 200.

1317. One gigabyte of storage cost $300,000 in 1981. Now it says cheap as 10 cents.

1318. Emotions and Stress can adversely affect your body. Negativity can actually lower your immune systems response against disease.

1319. In the 1930's, people lacking space in their London apartments used to utilize a baby cage for more space and for fresh air for their babies.

1320. The word dinosaur comes from the ancient Greek words, deinos, meaning fearfully-great, as in awe inspiring, and sauros, meaning lizard. The name was invented in 1842 by Richard Owen.

1321. The jaguar is the national animal of Brazil. It's scientific name is Panthera onca and is the largest carnivorous mammal in Central and South America weighing up to 211 pounds.

1322. In 2013, scientists from the University of Chile have spent a year designing a new vaccine that will give anyone who drinks even a small amount of alcohol an immediate, very bad hangover. They developed it to help tackle the problem of alcoholism in the country.

1323. The sloth only urinates and defecates once a week. Constipation is normal for them, and so, when they do go, it's like giving birth. Their poop comes out looking like a long piece of rotten banana.

1324. In North Korea, only military and government officials can own motor vehicles.

1325. Before there was modern refrigeration, people in Russia and Finland put Russian brown frogs in their milk to keep it fresh. According to Moscow State University organic chemist, A. T. Lebedev, the frog's skin secretions are loaded with peptides and anti-microbial compounds.

1326. The Blue Whale has the highest percentage of body fat of any animal at more than 35%. Whales can weigh up to 180 tonnes which means upto 63 tonnes of fat.

1327. In the movie 'Saving Private Ryan', directors depicted combat so realistically that veterans actually had to leave the theaters during the opening scene stating that it was the most realistic depiction of combat that they had ever seen.

1328. A 14-carat gold Lego brick was given out in the early 80s to employees who had worked at the Germany Lego Factory for over 25 years. They are valued at over $15,000.

1329. Pineapples were considered a status symbol in the 18th century. They were seen as a symbol of wealth and power, and in England, people were able to rent one for a night to show off to partygoers.

1330. We generally don't think of food as too sweet until our bones stop growing. This is why kids tend to like sweets a lot more than adults do.

1331. A wild pig in Australia once stole 18 beers from some campers, got drunk, and then got into a fight with a cow.

1332. Philip A. Contos was a motorcyclist who died at an anti-helmet rally after he flipped over his handlebars and hit his head on the pavement.

1333. The Incas measured their units of time by how long it would take to cook a potato.

1334. MI-5 once had a plan to use gerbils to detect terrorists and spies at airports. This is because their sense of smell can acutely detect increased adrenaline in people, but the project was scrapped when the gerbils proved unable to tell the difference between terrorists and those who were just afraid of flying.

1335. In 2004, Google anonymously posted math equations on billboards in Harvard Square and Silicon Valley that, if solved, led to a website with another equation, which in turn, allowed you to submit your resume.

1336. In Sweden, it is illegal to name your baby Metallica, Superman, Veranda, Ikea or Elvis.

1337. On August 16, 1996, at the Brookfield Zoo, a three-year-old boy fell into a gorilla enclosure and lost consciousness, but Binti Jua, a female gorilla, guarded the young boy from other gorillas, cradled him in her arms, and carried him to an entrance where zookeepers could actually retrieve him.

1338. Studies conducted by the global commission on aging at Transamerica Center for Retirement Studies show that traveling is good for you. It promotes brain health and decreases your risk of heart attack and depression.

1339. Compared to one cigarette, one hookah session delivers about 25 times the tar, 2.5 times the nicotine and 10 times the carbon monoxide.

1340. In 2009 three masked burglars unknowingly broke into Swedish actor Dolph Lundgren's home, tied him up and then threatened his wife. But they immediately fled when they found a family photo and realized who owned the home.

1341. It took Ronda Rousey a total of only 25 minutes and thirty-six seconds to win all of her 12 fights.

1342. Bowhead whales are amongst the longest-living mammals. In 2007, a specimen caught off the Alaskan coast was found to have a 35-inch-long head of an explosive harpoon embedded deep in its neck. The projectile was manufactured in Massachusetts around 1890, suggesting that the whale survived a hunt over a century ago.

1343. Humpback whales often let dolphins hitch a ride on their head for the sheer fun of it.

1344. The difference between terror and horror is that terror occurs in anticipation of the horrifying experience, while horror occurs after.

1345. Your eyebrows renew themselves every 64 days.

1346. Five high school students and their teacher from a small town in Sicily, Italy, created a prototype of a vending machine that turns your plastic recyclables into phone cases. It grinds down the plastics into tiny pellets which are then melted and then used to create 3D printed phone cases. The project was created to encourage other youths to recycle more.

1347. Retired NBA All-Star basketball player, Yao Ming, has his own winery in Napa Valley. Yao Family Wines opened in 2009 and makes ultra-premium wines and is open from 10 to five for tastings.

1348. In late 2016, the world's second tallest building, the Shanghai Tower, built the world's fastest elevator. According to manufacturer, Mitsubishi, the elevator moves as fast as 4,035 feet (1200 meters) per minute. That's 46 miles (76 km) per hour.

1349. Steven Tyler, from the band Aerosmiths, birth name was Steven Victor Tallarico.

1350. Sushi is actually meant to be eaten with your hands and sashimi with chopsticks.

1351. Before Saladin, the first Sultan of Egypt died in 1193. He had given all of his wealth to his poor subjects. His final estate consisted of a single piece of gold and 40 pieces of silver, not even enough to pay for the funeral.

1352. KevJumba, a YouTuber, created a second YouTube channel and donated 100% of its ad revenue to a community in Kenya which used that money to construct the first secondary school in their community and named the school after him.

1353. Breastfeeding allows the baby to give germs to the mother so her immune system can respond and synthesize antibodies for her baby.

1354. Jason Padgett was a jock who never made it past pre-Algebra, but, after being attacked outside of a bar, he started seeing the world in pixelated, geometric shapes. He soon understood the concept of pi, and had a sudden ability to hand draw complex fractals and is now a renowned math genius.

1355. A Florida woman named Sara Barnes accidentally burned down a 3,500-year-old cypress tree. It was the fifth oldest in the country, and she did it because she was smoking meth under it and lit a fire so that she could see her meth better.

1356. The town of Tikrit in Iraq erected a two-meter-tall monument to the shoe that was thrown by the journalist at George W. Bush during his final visit to Iraq.

1357. A bear named Wojtek, which means he who enjoys war, fought in the Polish army in World War II. He carried shells to the front line and was taught to salute and even became a mascot for the soldiers. Although he developed a habit for drinking beer and smoking cigarettes, he survived the war and lived the rest of his life in the Edinburgh Zoo.

1358. Limbo queen Shemika Charles had been training six hours a day since she was a teenager. She set a world record in 2010 and is now so flexible that she could actually limbo under a car.

1359. In 2015, Adidas released a shoe made entirely from ocean trash, including gill nets and beach litter. The company stated that there is no shortage of material to produce this line.

1360. When the mummified remains of Ramses II was transported in 1974, it was issued an Egyptian passport, which listed his occupation as king deceased.

1361. A study done in 2011 shows that the brain responds to emotional pain the same way that it does to physical pain. So when people say rejection hurts, it's quite true

1362. When Thor: The Dark World came out, a movie theater in Shanghai accidentally used a fan-made photo as the official poster for the film.

1363. UK brothers Jeff and John Bitmead created a grown-up version of the red and yellow Little Tikes toy car. It's road legal, fully functional, and can go up to 370 feet (113 kilometers) an hour.

1364. Mice can sing just like birds. It's simply inaudible to human ears.

1365. Queen Elizabeth II has owned more than 30 Corgis over her reign.

1366. Steve Jobs had a high school GPA of 2.65.

1367. Hummingbirds have such a high metabolism that they are always hours away from starving to death.

1368. In France, it is illegal for grocery stores to throw away edible food. Stores have to donate edible, unused food to charity or facilities that process it into animal feed or compost.

1369. A survey conducted by 'Buy T-Shirts Online' says that those who wear black are seen as serious and reliable. Almost 50% of women and 64% of men agree that black exudes confidence.

1370. Lois Gibson is the world's most successful police sketch artist. By being patient and talking to victims she's able to coax out realistic descriptions of the suspects. At last count back in 2007 she'd helped solve over 1,000 cases in Texas alone, in the 30 years that she'd been in the police force.

1371. In 1893, the first graduating class of New Mexico State University had one student. His name was Sam Steele and he was murdered before graduation.

1372. In developing countries, beehive fences are used to deter elephants by taking advantage of their natural fear of bees, and they worked. They have reduced conflicts between humans and elephants by over 80%.

1373. The University of Oxford is so old that one of its constituent colleges New College was actually established in 1379.

1374. Bamboo is the fastest growing plant in the world. It can grow up to 91 centimeters in a single day.

1375. Because he didn't like to sign autographs, Marlon Brando's personal checks became collector's items. People often didn't cash Brando's checks because his signature was worth more than the checks were made out for.

1376. There is an environmentally friendly spray-on coating for pavements called Star Path that makes pavement glow in the dark. Not only that, but it even adjusts to the level of natural light available and the darker it is the brighter it glows.

1377. Ducks have accents. Just like humans they're influenced by their environment and this affects their communication making them quack in regional accents.

1378. At 52, Rolling Stones bassist Bill Wyman married 18 year old Mandy Smith, but divorced after a year. Bill's 30 year old son Stephen then married Mandy's mother, age 46. If Bill and Mandy had remained married, Stephen would have been his father's father-in-law, and his own grandpa.

1379. The Gobi chimpanzee war was a conflict between the two communities of chimpanzees in Tanzania that lasted four years and included violent skirmishes, numerous deaths, and kidnappings.

1380. If your friend has a hard time waking up, there's a sonic grenade alarm clock that might just do the trick. Just pull the pin, toss it into their room, and run for cover. It emits an ear splitting noise that they can't turn off until you decide to put the pin back in.

1381. Voyager II was launched on August 20, 1977, and Voyager I was launched September 5th. They were sent on different trajectories and Voyager I was put on a path to reach Jupiter and Saturn ahead of Voyager II.

1382. Canada is larger than the entire European Union. In fact, it's 33 times bigger than Italy and 15 times bigger than France.

1383. If you have a fear of cheese, you have something called turophobia.

1384. In order to get street view of a desert, Google hires camels to carry its trekker camera. The term Captcha stands for Completely Automated Public Turing Test to tell Computers And Humans Apart.

1385. Scorpions glow a bright blue green when under ultraviolet light.

1386. According to National Geographic, there used to be 100,000 wild tigers in Asia a century ago; now due to poaching, sadly there are only about 3,200.

1387. According to a report by Michael Gibson Light, a doctoral candidate in the University of Arizona's School of Sociology, ramen noodles are now more popular than tobacco as currency in U.S. prisons.

1388. The owner of the Gin Tub in Brighton, England had a faraday cage built into its ceiling to block cell phone reception. He wants his patrons to socialize the old-fashioned way.

1389. There are no natural lakes in the state of Maryland. All of the lakes are man-made by damming rivers.

1390. According to Guinness World Records, the only man to be struck by lightning seven times was ex park ranger Roy C. Sullivan. He suffered a lost toenail, lost eyebrows, a shoulder injury, leg burns, an ankle injury, chest and stomach burns, and had his hair set on fire twice. Unfortunately, he ended up taking his own life after being rejected in love.

1391. Jupiter's largest moon, Ganymede, has a saltwater ocean buried under 95 miles (152 km) of ice. Scientists estimate that it's 60 miles (96 km) thick, which is about 10 times deeper than our oceans.

1392. After trick photography was developed in 1856, creating headless portraits became a trend that swept through the Victorian era.

1393. The box jellyfish's venom is among the most deadly in the world. Human victims sometimes drown of heart failure from the pain and shock and survivors can continue feeling considerable pain for weeks after. They also often have significant scarring where the tentacle made contact with their bodies.

1394. Flowers from bamboo are rarely seen. Some species can develop flowers after 65 to 120 years. But, what's most fascinating, is that if they do flower, all plants of that one bamboo species develop flowers at the same time no matter where they're located in the world.

1395. Gasoline, kerosene, benzine, and turpentine all used to be used to cure head lice. References to it appear in medical journals as far back as 1917.

1396. Antarctica has no reptiles. Reptiles need heat to keep their bodies functioning, so they cannot survive in severe, extended cold temperatures. They would literally freeze solid.

1397. There's an island in Brazil that is untouched by humans because it is covered in deadly snakes. The Ilha da Queimada Grande, or Snake Island, has up to five golden lancehead snakes per square meter. The golden lancehead is responsible for 90% of snake bite related fatalities in Brazil. The snakes are so dangerous that the Navy has forbidden anyone from landing there.

1398. There's an underwater museum off the coast of the Spanish island of Lanzarote called Museo Atlantico. It contains the sculptures of British artist, Jason deCaires Taylor, and depicts our changing, and sometimes destructive, role in the modern world.

1399. Mark Spitz, 9 time Olympic champion, jokingly told the Russian swim team coach in 1972 that his mustache increased his speed in the water, deflecting water away from his mouth. The next year every Russian swimmer was sporting a mustache.

1400. There's an aquarium in Japan called Keikyu Aburatsubo Marine Park, where they let you shake hands with otters.

1401. Greenland allows its inmates huge liberties as part of its open prison system, aimed to rehabilitate prisoners. Inmates are allowed to leave the premises during the day for work or school and even go hunting with rifles. Believe it or not, some of them even hold the key to their own cell.

1402. The world's ugliest animal is the Blobfish. A deep-sea fish that can live anywhere between 2000 and 4000 feet (600 and 1200 meters) below water, because of its lack of flesh and muscle structure.

1403. According to a study conducted in 2012, people who complain actually live longer by about two years. This is because by complaining they release their tension which increases their immunity and boosts their health.

1404. In 2014 an entrepreneur named Muchi Tsung developed a facial recognition software for cats. It's aimed to help cats maintain their goal weight by recognizing their faces and tracking their food intake.

1405. In 2008 as part of a fundraiser, Father Adelir de Carle of Brazil, tied 1,000 balloons to an armchair in an attempt to break the world record for the most hours flying with balloons. Unfortunately the winds blew him off course and he lost contact with the ground.

1406. Studies show that just one week of camping outdoors with only natural light is enough to reset the body's biological clock to normal sleep rhythms.

1407. The tesla model S car aced all of its national highway traffic safety tests. In fact it's so safe that it actually broke the crash testing gear.

1408. Lillian Weber is a woman from Iowa who makes a dress from scratch every single day so that a child in need can have something beautiful to wear. She has made over 840 dresses in the last several years for an organization called little dresses for Africa.

1409. In 2014 scientists at MIT designed a device to help the blind read without braille. It's called the finger reader, and wearers can use it to scan a line of text with their finger and receive audio feedback of the words.

1410. In order to advertise their services, prostitutes in ancient Greece wore sandals that left the words follow me imprinted in the dirt as they walked.

1411. On the evening of September 11, 2001, hundreds of Iranian people gathered in Madar Square, Tehran, in a candlelight vigil to express sympathy and support for the American people.

1412. There are more neurons lining your stomach than there are in your spinal cord, so your digestive system can work without needing your brain. In fact when you're flooded with emotion the neurons react and you get a gut feeling.

1413. 29 year old Alasan Dixon from Ireland has mastered the art of the animal selfie. Though they appear very casual he sometimes spends hours gaining an animal's trust before a shot.

1414. Despite being a millionaire Steve Jobs only paid $500 a month in child support to his daughter Lisa. That's the same girl that he named the computer after, but still attempted to deny paternity for.

1415. In 1986 Soviet pilot Alexander Kliuyev made a bet with a copilot that he could land an airplane blind. He curtained the cockpit windows and crashed the plane into a landing strip killing 70 out of 87 passengers.

1416. There's a battery powered bell at Oxford University that has been continuously ringing for over 175 years. Nobody knows what the battery is composed of and no one wants to take the device apart in order to figure it out.

1417. The 'Like-A-Hug' jacket gives you a hug whenever a friend likes one of your Facebook posts.

1418. In World War II nine airmen escaped from their planes after being shot down during bombing raids. Eight out of the nine men were captured, tortured, beheaded and eaten. The ninth man was George W. Bush.

1419. In 2015 a man named Torkel Kristoffers was arrested for kidnapping when his neighbors didn't recognize him with his new beard that he grew while taking time off of work.

1420. Studies have suggested that gifted people often have bad handwriting because their brains are often working faster than their hand.

1421. There's a biological reason why we can't resist puppy dog eyes. Sustained eye contact significantly raises oxytocin levels in both humans and dogs, which in turn encourages trust, love, and bonding. This response isn't found in even hand raised wolves, which suggests that humans and dogs may have co-evolved to share this trait in order to be companions.

1422. In Finland, speeding tickets are calculated on a percentage of the person's income. This causes some Finnish millionaires to face fines of over $100,000.

1423. Nobody has died from a confirmed spider bite in Australia since 1979. Deaths by spiders actually occur more from being surprised by them, like while you're driving.

1424. Psychopaths are immune to contagious yawning and are less likely to be startled.

1425. Yunessun Spa House in Hakone, a southeastern town in Japan, is now offering ramen noodle baths. The bath, consisting of ramen pork broth and synthetic noodles allegedly helps improve patient's skin.

1426. Colonel Sanders would often make surprise visits to KFC restaurants. If he was dissatisfied with the food, he would throw it on the ground and curse at the employees.

1427. Alzheimer's disease does not affect emotional memory as strongly as informational memory. As a result, Alzheimer's patients, when given bad news, will quickly forget the news but will remain sad and have no idea why.

1428. There is a popular tourist destination in Chongqing, China, where part of the pavement is devoted to cellphone users who are too busy looking at their screens to bother looking where they're going. Right beside it is another section of the road that completely bans the use of cell phones.

1429. There's an island in Alaska that's reflected in such a way that it looks like it's just floating in air.

1430. Route 50 in the United States is also known as the loneliest road in America because of the large desolate areas the road goes through.

1431. The most important organism in the world is marine algae because it produces about 70 to 80 percent of our oxygen.

1432. The word electrocute comes from the combination of electro and execute meaning death by electric shock. So technically if you survive an electric shock you aren't electrocuted but just shocked.

1433. When filming Mission Impossible, Tom Cruise vandalized the world's tallest building. He climbed to the top of the Burj Khalifa and etched his then wife's name, Katie Holmes, into the spire.

1434. Peacock flounders are masters of camouflage and can match the color of a checkerboard if they are placed on one.

1435. The FedEx logo has won over 40 design awards and was ranked as one of the 8 best logos in the last 35 years. And in case you never noticed it, the white arrow in the logo was an intentional design choice, crafted by blending two different fonts together.

1436. Steve Jobs' biological father was a Syrian immigrant.

1437. Women have twice as many nerve receptors as men, causing them to feel pain more intensely. However, they also have a higher tolerance for it.

1438. Meteors were initially only referred to as comets, a name given from the Latin word "comes" meaning hair, and were given their name for the flowing golden tail of hair that flashed through the sky.

1439. According to studies conducted at Turkey's Ataturk University and the University of Manchester, dogs and cats are right and left pawed, just like humans are right and left handed.

1440. If you could dig a hole through the earth and jump through it without dying, you would not come out the other side. You would fall down for 20 minutes until you reached the center, then technically, you would be considered falling up until you made it to the opposite surface. However, if no one was there to catch you, you would fall down again over and over forever.

1441. Prior to the invention of rubber erasers in 1770 by Edward Nairne, people would use moist bread to erase pencil marks. In fact, the invention of the eraser, which fixes mistakes, was discovered by accident by Edward thinking that he had grabbed bread.

1442. Henry Cavill almost missed the call for the role of Superman from Zack Snyder because he was playing World of Warcraft.

1443. A study published by the Journal of Transportation found that people are in the best mood when they are bicycling compared to any other mode of transportation.

1444. There exists a variation of soccer where three teams face off against each other at the same time.

1445. The tallest outdoor elevator in the world is the Bailong Elevator, also known as the Hundred Dragons Elevator. It carries tourists 1,083 feet (330 meters) up the side of a massive sandstone column in a mountain range in China's Hunan Province. It's so big that it can carry 50 people at a time.

1446. Britain is responsible for creating the lie that carrots improve eyesight, to distract the Nazis of a new technology that they made for night raids.

1447. Frank Hayes, an American jockey, suffered a fatal heart attack in 1923 and died mid-race. His body remained on the horse and crossed the finish line in first place. He had never won a race before in his life.

1448. Studies from the University of Chicago concluded that lonely people spend more time in their beds regardless of whether they're tired or not. Chronic loneliness can cause insomnia as well as the need to get in bed without feeling tired.

1449. Rick Astley became an Internet phenomenon in 2007 with his video "Never Gonna Give You Up" when it became part of an Internet prank known as "Rickrolling". Sadly, he forgot to claim ownership of his work, and earned only $12 in royalties off of his nearly 150 million YouTube views.

1450. In the Vietnamese version of Cinderella, "Tam Cam", Cinderella dismembers her stepsister, puts the body into a jar of food, and sends it to her stepmother to eat, who enjoys it until she finds a skull at the bottom of the jar, and then dies out of shock.

1451. A "gut feeling" is actually a chemical signal that your stomach creates to warn your brain of danger.

1452. Starting in 1979, the residents of Naco, Arizona and Naco, Mexico began an annual tradition of having a volleyball match over the fence of the border that divides them.

1453. Thomas Jefferson proposed in 1784 to end slavery in all the territories, but his bill was lost in Congress by a single vote.

1454. In Texas, it is against the law for anyone to have a pair of pliers in their possession.

1455. Praying mantises can turn their heads 180 degrees. They use this ability to scan their surroundings using two large, compound eyes and three other simple eyes located between them.

1456. When minimum wage first became a law in the U.S. back in 1938, it was 25 cents an hour and if you adjust that for inflation, it would be $4.31 cents an hour today.

1457. New York's first Saint Patrick's Day parade was held on March 17th, 1762.

1458. On March 13th, 1781, astronomer William Herschel discovered the planet Uranus. It was the first discovery to be made in modern times and also the first to be made using a telescope.

1459. On July 16th, 1935, the world's first parking meter, known as the Park-O-Meter, was installed on the southeast corner of what was then First Street and Robinson Avenue in Oklahoma City.

1460. Panama hats are actually made in Ecuador, not Panama.

1461. Actor Tommy Lee Jones and Vice President Al Gore were freshmen roommates at Harvard.

1462. Adidas will cancel any sponsorship deal that they have with a player if it turns out he has anything to do with Scientology.

1463. "Puppy Pregnancy Syndrome" is an illness where the sufferer believes that they are pregnant with puppies after being bitten by a dog.

1464. The Yakuza, Japan's largest organized crime syndicate, provided food, water, blankets, diapers and more during both the 1995 and 2001 Japanese earthquakes. They even had a faster response time than the Japanese government.

1465. Doodlebug is an orphaned baby kangaroo that was found abandoned on the side of the road when he walked up to a human, held up his arms and asked to be picked up. The rescuer later gave him a teddy bear, and he wouldn't stop hugging it.

1466. Jets leave a white trail across the sky for the same reason that you can see your breath in the winter. It's carbon dioxide and water creating visible moisture.

1467. The sixth-tallest pyramid in the world is a Bass Pro Shops mega store, located in Memphis, Tennessee.

1468. White supremacist and racist Craig Cobb said that he would take a genetic test and receive the results on live television. He was found to be 14% Sub-Saharan African.

1469. A man named László Polgár developed a method to raise child prodigies. He wrote a book on it, married a language teacher, and they raised the world's best and second-best chess players.

1470. In 2014, a fan was waving a flare at a Polish soccer game when a security guard used pepper spray on him, not knowing that the substances were combustible, causing him to burst into flames.

1471. German canoeist Oskar Speck kayaked from Germany to Australia between 1932 and 1939, only to arrive to be declared as a prisoner of war due to the outbreak of World War II.

1472. Scientists at the University of South Denmark have created "Aquaman crystals" that can actually absorb a roomful of oxygen and store it for later use. This discovery might actually be the key to underwater breathing. A handful of crystals could pull oxygen from the water and provide divers with air.

1473. Killer whales that live in captivity with dolphins can learn their complicated language and they eventually actually begin to use it.

1474. Harvard is officially free for those with less than $65,000 in annual family income. You still need to get the marks to get in however.

1475. If a catastrophe or hacking group caused the Internet to crash, there are seven people in the world who have key cards that can reboot the system when five of the keys are used together. They literally hold the keys to the worldwide Internet security.

1476. Researchers at Ohio State University have discovered something that they're calling experience talking. It's where, while reading a book or story, people actually change their behavior or thoughts to match those of a fictional character in a book or story that they can identify with. They subconsciously become that character.

1477. The life expectancy of people with Down syndrome has increased from 25 in 1983 to 60 today.

1478. According to research done by Aric Prather, assistant professor of psychiatry at The University of California, you are four times more likely to get a cold if you get less than six hours of sleep per night.

1479. Actor Tom Cruise is only 5.6 feet tall.

1480. Biologists led by Koji Nishida at Osaka University in Japan have discovered a new way to grow parts of the human eye, like the retina, cornea and lens just by using a small sample of adult skin.

1481. According to a study done in 2013 by researchers at The Harvard School of Public Health, drinking several cups of coffee daily appears to reduce the risk of suicide in men and women by about 50%.

1482. U.S. politician, Henry Kissinger, was the person who convinced Brazilian soccer great Pele, to play in The United States.

1483. In 1140, when King Conrad III of Germany captured a castle, the women of the castle were granted free departure and allowed to take what they could carry on their backs. Thinking quickly, the women often carried the men on their backs. The king kept his word and let the men leave that way.

1484. The female loggerhead turtle will sometimes travel thousands of kilometers to return to the beach where they hatch their eggs.

1485. In 1978, serial killer Rodney Alcala, who murdered four women and a child, appeared on a game show The Dating Game and won.

1486. White House physician, Admiral Joel T. Boone, invented a game called Hoover-Ball for President Hoover. It was a combination of tennis, volleyball and medicine ball created to help keep President Hoover physically fit.

1487. All 10 of the documented people that lived the longest are all women, each range from 116 years old to 122 years old.

1488. The plane that crashed in the movie The Dark Knight Rises with the use of computer generated special effects actually did crash the next year, killing two people on board.

1489. The word emoji is the Japanese term for picture characters. Emojis were actually born out of necessity back in 1999, when mobile carriers were struggling to support the messaging needs of 80 million users of a rapidly growing technology of cell phones, and their hopes were that an emoji would reduce the need for multiple text messages or even picture messages.

1490. Blue jays and cardinals go bald in the late summer and fall. Usually they lose all of their feathers and replace them gradually when they mount, but sometimes they lose them all at once, creating a bald head. They're only bald for about a week though, and their feathers grow back.

1491. Actress Carrie Mulligan and singer Marcus Mumford of Mumford & Sons were childhood pen pals who lost contact. Each individually found fame and were reintroduced to each other as adults and fell in love.

1492. Results from an online survey revealed that 11% of Americans think that HTML is a type of STD.

1493. In 1859, English settler Thomas Austin released 24 rabbits onto his property in Australia, stating the introduction of a few rabbits could do little harm and might provide a touch of home in addition to a spot of hunting. By the 1920s, the rabbit population had reached 10 billion.

1494. There's a place in California called glass beach, where years of people dumping garbage into an area of the coastline has resulted in the development of smooth sea glass. Believe it or not tourists in the area like to collect the glass, so now there's actually been a movement to replenish the beach with discarded glass.

1495. Architects in Australia design a concept home called the cliff house. The concept shows a five-story house hanging off a cliff on the australian south west coast with amazing views of the Indian ocean.

1496. Germany is a graveyard for unexploded bombs left over world war two. Disturbingly, an average of 2,000 tons of buried munitions are discovered there annually.

1497. The Charbonnet Labatt funeral home became famous in 2014, for displaying the bodies of the deceased in upright poses. Disturbingly the phenomenon of the sitting dead actually first appeared in 2008 in Puerto Rico.

1498. Apple generated $43.7 billion in sales in the first quarter of 2014 which was more than Google, Amazon, and Facebook combined.

1499. The Hawaiian island Niihau is also known as the forbidden island. Elizabeth Sinclair bought it in 1864 and now her descendants the Robinson family own it. The island is completely off-limits to everyone except the island owners, relatives, and invited guests.

1500. Even though we're laughing when we're being tickled, it's actually our body's defense mechanism kicking into gear in responding to panic and anxiety.

1501. Madagascar houses some of the most exotic organisms on the planet. About 90% of all plant and animal species found in Madagascar are endemic, meaning that they're unique to a specific geographical location

1502. During the first world war, there was a Christmas truce in 1914. In the week leading up to Christmas German and British soldiers had a series of cease-fires where they entered No-man's land to mingle and exchange seasonal greetings. That truce is seen as a symbolic moment of peace during one of the most violent events in history.

1503. In 2012, more than 30% of all deaths in Russia were attributed to alcohol.

1504. Herders in Finland spray reindeer's antlers with a reflective paint, so that they won't cause as many traffic accidents.

1505. In 2011, after four years of planning, in two months, working every night from 10 PM to 5 AM, a team of hackers at MIT actually turned their Earth and Planetary Science Department building into a giant, multicolored, playable Tetris game.

1506. During the Vietnam War, American troops would eat small amounts of C4 plastic explosive in order to get high.

1507. Virtually all of the eyewear industry is controlled by one Italian company: Luxottica SpA, which owns brands such as Ray-Ban, Persol, and Oakley. They also make glasses for Chanel, Prada, Armani, Burberry, Versace, Dolce Gabanna, and a lot more. They also own retail brands like LensCrafters and Sears Optical.

1508. The very first message sent between two computers over the Internet was back in 1969, and it was "lo". It was supposed to be "login", but the computer crashed after the first two letters.

1509. Skeleton flowers have such delicate petals that they become transparent when it rains.

1510. Having bridesmaids in a wedding wasn't originally for moral support. They were actually intended to confuse evil spirits or those who wished harm on the bride.

1511. About 70% of the world's spice production comes from one country, India.

1512. New York City has the area code 212 because rotary phones were used at the time, and the number uses the shortest dialing time.

1513. In January of 2013, the finance minister of Zimbabwe announced that his country had only 217 dollars left in its bank account.

1514. Mike Tyson was arrested a whopping 38 times by the time that he was 13 years old. He was sent to a boy's home where he found out that he could box and he started training professionally with a former boxer and the rest is history.

1515. There's a charity organization called Food for the Poor that gives over 95% of their proceeds to the poor. Ironically their CEO's name is Robin Mahfood.

1516. Marie Antoinette's last words were, Monsieur, I beg your pardon. She was apologizing to her executioner after she accidentally stepped on his foot on the way to the guillotine.

1517. Humans are the kings of the planet when it comes to long-distance running. We can outrun every animal on the planet and run in conditions that no other animal can run in.

1518. Forty-two-year-old Russian fisherman Igor Vorozhbitsyn was brutally attacked by a bear, but he was suddenly saved when his ringtone, that his granddaughter installed on his phone, Justin Bieber's 'Baby', went off, sending the bear running back into the woods.

1519. The word "outlaw" originally meant outside the protection of the law, so you could rob or kill them without legal consequences.

1520. At the Nuremberg trials, several Nazi leaders achieved genius level scores of an IQ test.

1521. When 70-year-old farmer Winston Howe's wife of 33 years Janet died suddenly he decided that he wanted to create a lasting tribute to her, so he planted thousands of oak saplings in a six acre field and left a heart shaped point facing towards her childhood home.

1522. Villagers in the Indian village of Marottichal began playing chess as an alternative to drinking after a ban on alcohol. The village is now known as Chess Village due to its near 100% chess literacy.

1523. Japan keeps a defunct train station called Kyu-Shirataki on the island of Hokkaido running just for one girl, so that she can attend school every day. The train only makes two stops. One when the lone high-school student leaves for school and the other when she returns.

1524. A typical Rihanna hit single costs around $75,000 to make, another million to promote it, but the lyrics are usually written in about 15 minutes.

1525. In 539 BC, Persian king Cyrus the Great issued the first ever decree on human rights. He freed the slaves, declared that all people had the right to choose their own religion, and established racial equality.

1526. Crack dealing is one of the most dangerous jobs in America, and the salary on average is only about $3.30 an hour.

1527. Hitler actually had a pet alligator named Saturn, now aged 85 that Russians were gifted by the British government. Saturn is actually still alive and well, and can be seen at the Moscow Zoo.

1528. There are a total of 15 countries with absolutely no military force including Costa Rica, Liechtenstein and Samoa.

1529. Author Peter Benchley, who wrote Jaws, was the first-ever host of Shark Week. In the years since, MythBusters star Adam Savage, Dirty Jobs host Mike Rowe, late night host Craig Ferguson and former SNL star Andy Samberg have all filled the role.

1530. Colorado-based company Apollo Peak has created a wine for cats. It actually contains no alcohol and is made of catnip with beets to give it that red wine color. It comes in flavors like pinot meow and moscato. Single serving bottles are $5, and eight-ounce bottles are $12.

1531. In July of 2016, monks from Prince Edward Island, Canada, went all around the island buying up to 600 pounds of lobster just to release them back into the ocean. The purpose was to cultivate compassion for the lobsters and for all beings.

1532. You can buy a fan just for your armpits. Japanese gadget-maker Thanko has developed the wacky gadget. It's a battery-run small fan that clips onto your sleeve to deliver cool air to your armpits for five to nine hours, but if that isn't long enough, you can actually connect it to your PC or a battery pack.

1533. Since 1996, Harold Hackett from Prince Edward Island, Canada, has launched 4,871 messages in a bottle into the ocean and has actually received 3,100 responses. That's a 63.6% response rate.

1534. Paris only has one stop sign. Every intersection in Paris is basically a mad free-for-all where you enter at your own risk.

1535. In German there's something called Street Pong where there are touch screens installed on traffic lights so you can play pong with people across the street from you.

1536. Research shows from 2014 that sleep patterns are linked with important character traits and behavior and that people who stay up late tend to take more risks than early risers.

1537. Only one person has ever been killed by armed police in Iceland since it became an independent republic in 1944.

1538. Anything that a duckling meets within the first 10 minutes after it's born will consider its parent forever.

1539. Early on in Beyoncé's career, she was managed by her father, Matthew Knowles. He would make his daughter and the other members of Destiny's Child run a mile while singing so that they could perform on stage without getting exhausted.

1540. In 1969, Bill Cosby won a Man of the Year Award and jokingly suggested renaming the award to "The Nice Guy As Far As We Know Award".

1541. In 2007, Harry Potter star Daniel Radcliffe wore the same clothes home from a theater in London for six months in a row so that the paparazzi would end up with the same photos every day and therefore not be able to publish the pictures.

1542. Sometimes female lions can develop manes. Such masculine females likely occur when the embryo is disrupted either at conception or while in the womb.

1543. Engineers in Canada receive an iron ring to remind them to have humility. It's in memory of a bridge that collapsed twice due to incorrect calculations involving iron.

1544. The 'your mother' insult is found in nearly all cultures and is as old as humanity itself, with examples in Shakespeare and the Bible.

1545. Mobile phone throwing is a sport in Finland.

1546. Dwayne "The Rock" Johnson released a motivational alarm clock. He created the app to help you get out of bed and meet your personal goals and the best thing is that there is no snooze button. There are 25 ringtones to choose from that were created by The Rock himself. For example, there's one that's just a mash up of sounds that come from his dog, a couple where he just keeps repeating the words beep and ring-ring, and another where he smashes a harp.

1547. The world's biggest tire graveyard is in Sulaibiya, Kuwait. Every single year, gigantic holes are dug into the desert and filled with old tires. There are seven million tires there already and the dump is so large that it's actually visible from space.

1548. There's a monument in Israel called the "9/11 Living Memorial Plaza" that was initiated and designed by Eliezer Weishoff. It was completed in 2009 for $2 million and sits on a hill overlooking Jerusalem's largest cemetery. It's a 30-foot bronze American flag that forms the shape of a flame to commemorate the flames of the Twin Towers. The base of it is made from melted steel from the wreckage of the original World Trade Center. Surrounding the monument are plaques with the names of the victims of 9/11.

1549. In 2015, Disney banned the use of selfie sticks in their parks due to safety concerns. Gadgets were already prohibited on rides, but selfie sticks themselves pose a unique concern, as the long arms could collide with a ride's mechanism or stick another guest.

1550. Swindon, England, is home to what may be the most confusing-looking intersection ever created. The 'Magic Roundabout' was designed by engineer Frank Blackmore of the British Transport and Road Research Laboratory back in 1972 to help alleviate traffic jams. The interchange consists of five separate smaller roundabouts supporting clockwise traffic; all situated around one larger central roundabout that runs counterclockwise. Believe it or not, traffic jams were greatly reduced.

1551. The biggest stadium in the world is the Rungrado May Day Stadium, located in Pyongyang, North Korea. Completed on May 1st, 1989, it's used for sporting events but is more famous for being the place where the annual Mass Games are held, an artistic and gymnastic event with over 100,000 participants in it.

1552. Some of the world's oldest sunglasses were discovered on North Baffin Island in northern Canada. They were created by the Eskimo or Inuit of the Arctic. Also referred to as snow goggles, they were created from bone, leather, or wood, with small slits to see through, designed to protect the eyes from snow-blindness caused by the sun.

1553. 'Hatebeak' is a black metal band whose lead singer is a parrot.

1554. Wild dogs operate under a strict hierarchy while wolves will actually cooperate and communicate with each other to make decisions as a group.

1555. In 1990, disabled activists got out of their wheelchairs and crawled up the steps of the Capitol, inconveniencing senators to encourage a vote on the Americans with Disabilities Act.

1556. According to a study done in 2014 by St. Michael's Hospital, almost half of homeless men who took part in the study have suffered from at least one traumatic brain injury in their life. 87% of those injuries occurred before they lost their homes.

1557. Until 1992, it was not required for electrical appliances in Britain to be sold with plugs on the end of them. Often, consumers had to attach them themselves.

1558. Phil Collins' song 'Sussudio' was based on a completely made up word. When he couldn't think of actual lyrics to fill the line, he just left it in as the chorus and title.

1559. Troll dolls were originally created in 1959 by Danish fisherman and woodcutter Thomas Dam. Dam could not afford a Christmas gift for his daughter Lila and decided to carve a doll out of his own imagination. Other children in the Danish town of Gjøl, saw the troll doll and decided that they wanted one and the rest is history.

1560. Napoleon once removed the Mona Lisa from the Louvre so he could hang it on his bedroom wall.

1561. Coral is actually an animal, not a plant.

1562. Australian researchers at the Commonwealth Scientific and Industrial Research Organization discovered that drinking a cup of Asian pear juice before drinking alcohol resulted in fewer and/or diminished hangover symptoms the very next day.

1563. A stowaway Greek cat once flew in the undercarriage of an Airbus A321 from Athens to Zurich. It had shock and hypothermia but unbelievably it survived.

1564. The "PT" in PT Cruiser stands for Personal Transport.

1565. Samsung, the manufacturer of TVs, home appliances, and of course cell phones, started off as a grocery store.

1566. According to the National Severe Storms Laboratory, the part of lightning that we can see actually comes from the ground up, not the sky down.

1567. In 2011, a cafe opened in Istanbul called the Down Cafe. They only hire staff between the ages of 18 to 25 with Down syndrome.

1568. In 1891, Dr. James Naismith from Almonte, Ontario, Canada, invented the game of basketball. He cut out the bottom of a peach basket and hung it 10 feet in the air, and thus the game was born.

1569. In 2014, the International Space Station had to be moved three separate times in order to avoid being hit by lethal-sized space debris.

1570. Oregon's Mount Angel Abbey Museum houses the world's largest pig hairball. It's the size of a football.

1571. According to the New England Journal of Medicine, a 30-year-old man from India developed an unusual flower-shaped cataract with 10 petals after sustaining a concussion from a bike accident.

1572. In March of 2012, Israel adopted a law called the Photoshop Law, stipulating that fashion and commercial models should have a body mass index, or BMI, of at least 18.5. For context, a healthy BMI is between 18.5 to 24.9.

1573. Adding cold cream to your coffee actually keeps it warmer longer when compared to just black coffee.

1574. One in every 3,000 babies is born with a tooth.

1575. A study done in 2007 by the Bayer College of Medicine determined that magnesium, not calcium is the key to healthy bones.

1576. The Louvre Museum in Paris was the most visited museum in the world in 2014. There were 9.3 million visitors, almost the same amount of people as the population of Sweden.

1577. Approximately 1500 earthquakes are recorded in Japan every year.

1578. Seahorse babies eat as much as 3000 pieces of food a day. They have such a voracious appetite because they have no stomach and their digestive system has been described as inefficient, meaning that they must eat a lot in order to stay properly nourished.

1579. A frog's tongue is about a third of the length of its entire body. In comparison, if a human had the same sized tongue, it would reach our belly button.

1580. Researchers at the University of Oxford and the University of Queensland discovered that the small tropical archer fish can be taught to accurately recognize human faces. When the researchers display two faces side by side on a screen over a fish tank, one familiar and one unknown, the fish was able to recognize the same face 81% of the time in color and even more accurately in black and white images.

1581. Donald J Trump is the oldest U.S. president in history at almost 71 years old.

1582. Dolphins can't chew their food. Their teeth are only used to grip food and they'll shake and rub it on the ocean floor to tear it into smaller more manageable pieces.

1583. The Moomin House Cafe in Bunkyo, Tokyo offers coffee, treats, and companionship of an enormous stuffed animal. They will actually seat you with a stuffed animal so that you don't have to dine alone.

1584. In Singapore, the importation or sale of gum is illegal unless you have a medicinal reason for needing it.

1585. There's a solar facility at Walt Disney World in Lake Buena Vista, Florida that is comprised of 48,000 solar panels and is in the shape of Mickey Mouse.

1586. Researchers exploring the Northwestern Hawaiian Islands aboard the Okeanos Explorer came across the world's largest sea sponge. It was found 7000 feet (2100 meters) below the ocean surface and measured 12 feet long and seven feet wide.

1587. In 2015, in the French city of Valenciennes, a couple actually named their baby 'Nutella'. A judge ruled that it was contrary to the child's best interest to bear that name, as it was the name of a spread. When the parents failed to appear in court, they renamed the child 'Ella'.

1588. The average human scalp has 100,000 hair follicles.

1589. According to the American Psychological Association's 2014 survey, the most stressed out people in America are millennials, which are people between the ages of 18 and 35, women, parents with kids under 18, and low-income households. The main source of stress was money.

1590. The world's largest indoor beach is called the "Tropical Island Resort" in Krausnick, Germany. Built inside an old airplane hangar, it contains a 50,000-plant forest that spans over a 107,639-square-foot area, a spa, a waterfall, a whirlpool, and a water slide. In fact, it's big enough that you could fly a hot air balloon inside.

1591. There are hundreds of stone slabs dotting the coastlines of Japan that give advice. This advice includes "high dwellings are the peace and harmony of our descendants", "remember the calamity of the great tsunamis", "do not build any homes below this point" and also "if an earthquake comes, beware the tsunamis". Some of these markers are more than 600 years old.

1592. A handful of British companies are now offering "Pawternity", paid time off to take care of a pet in need.

1593. Over 3200 confirmed new planets have been discovered by telescope.

1594. London based ice cream company The Licktators, teamed up with breastfeeding campaigner Victoria Hilly to celebrate the birth of the royal baby number two by launching their breast milk flavored ice cream. The ice cream is called Royal Baby Gaga. It's made of donated breast milk that has been screened with hospital standards, and Madagascan vanilla.

1595. If you are caught injuring or killing a swan, or stealing one of their eggs in the UK, you could be fined or could be sent to jail for up to six months.

1596. South African architect Clara da Cruz Almeida has designed a little portable house that can be packed into a 258 square foot pod and shipped anywhere.

1597. Gladiators were for the most part, vegetarians. Their diets consisted of barley and vegetables. This enabled them to put on weight to protect them during fights and make them appear more spectacular to the crowd.

1598. Even though George Washington chose the site for the White House, he never actually lived there. In fact, he's the only president who did not reside in the White House.

1599. There's a gang of women called the Gulabi Gangor Pink Gang in India, who stand up to abusers in the country. The gang was founded in 2006, and is based in Badousa. It has a whopping 400,000 members, and helps bring rapists, abusers, and corrupt policemen to justice. The women that join the gang are registered, given a small ID card, and wear a distinctive pink uniform, a pink sari. And for 500 rupees a year, they also get a stick to carry.

1600. Lady Gaga has a whole genus of ferns named after her, a DNA sequence spells out Gaga, and the ferns have Gaga-like qualities. Some of them resemble her elaborate stage costumes, and one of them is even called the Gaga monstraparva.

1601. According to a team of astronomers and geologists led by J. Alexis Rodriguez, at the Planetary Science Institute in Tucson, Arizona, there is evidence that there were two massive tsunamis on Mars billions of years ago. They were both triggered by meteor impacts and were millions of years apart. They created waves as high as 150 feet (45 meters).

1602. The Hunger Games is banned in Vietnam. The movie was originally just delayed, but according to a member of the

Vietnamese National Film Board, the board considers the film to be too violent, and unanimously voted for it to be banned.

1603. Buzz Lightyear from Toy Story was actually named after astronaut Buzz Aldrin, the second astronaut to walk on the moon.

1604. The first Ferris Wheel was invented in 1893 for the Chicago World's Fair by George W. Ferris. It was 260 feet (79 m) high, cost 50 cents per ride, and could carry 60 passengers in each of the 36 cars. That's a total capacity of 2,160 passengers.

1605. In Alaska, it's against the law to look for a moose from an airplane.

1606. The two abbreviated letters 'OK' first appeared in the Boston Morning Post in March 23rd, 1839 as a joke. When it appeared in print, it was intended to be a shortening of "Orl Korrekt", the then humorous misspelling of all correct. It appeared in newspapers and in the 1840 presidential campaign, and after that, we continued to use it to this day.

1607. The highest flying bird in the world is the Ruffles Vulture. There is confirmed evidence of one flying at an altitude of 37,000 feet (11,300 meters) above sea level during which it collided with an aircraft.

1608. The Indianapolis 500 has claimed more than 60 lives, at least one of them being an innocent bystander. In 1931, a wreck by Billy Arnold sent a stray tire flying out of the race track and across the street where it struck and killed an 11 year old, Wilbur Brink, while he was playing in his front yard.

1609. In 1872, Victoria Woodhull was the first woman to vie for the presidency. She ran as an equal rights party nominee against Ulysses Grant. This was nearly 50 years before the 19th amendment gave women the right to vote.

1610. There's an exhibition at the Isle of Wight Zoo in the UK dedicated to poop. It features feces from the animal world and the human world. It also features fossilized poo called coprolites that dates back 140 million years.

1611. Up until 1564, the French celebrate New Years between March 25th and April 1st; but when the new Gregorian calendar was introduced, the festival was moved to January 1st. Those who resisted the change became victims of pranks, including invitations to non-existent New Year's parties on April 1st; and this is why we celebrate April Fool's Day on April 1st.

1612. According to a study done in 2007 by Marshall McCue, a researcher in the department of biological sciences at the University of Arkansas, intense snake hunger can cause snakes to actually digest their own heart muscle; however, immediately following a nutritious meal, snake hearts can actually quickly rebuild themselves.

1613. Some marine birds, like the penguin, have a supraorbital gland located just above their eyes that can remove sodium chloride from their blood stream. It works just like our kidneys, removing salt, which allows the penguin to survive without access to fresh water. The penguin excretes the salt byproduct as brine through its bill.

1614. In 2016, according to the brand management firm Interbrand's annual ranking of the best global brands, Apple was number one for the fourth year in a row, with a brand value of 178 billion, and Google was number two with a brand value of 133 billion.

1615. According to the Guinness World Records, the largest mouth in the world belonged to the bowhead whale. It can measure up to 16 feet long, 13 feet high, and eight feet wide. Its tongue alone weighs almost 2,000 pounds.

1616. The fastest recorded avalanche in history was the volcanic explosion of Mount St. Helens on May 18th, 1980. The velocity reached was 250 miles per hour.

1617. A study recently published in the journal of Neurobiology of Aging shows that the more flights of stairs a person climbs and the more years of school a person completes, the younger the brain physically looks. Researcher, Jason Steffener, a scientist at Concordia's PERFORM Centre, found that the brain age decreases by .95 years for each year of education, and it decreases 0.58 years for every daily flight of stairs climbed.

1618. Cornell University discovered that the tiger beetle runs so fast, it can no longer see where it's going. It actually has to use its antennae to avoid obstacles.

1619. New research published in the Journal of meteoritics and Planetary Science confirmed that the blade on the dagger found in Tutankhamun's tomb is made with materials from a meteorite. Scientists performed X-ray fluorescence spectrometry on it, which is a method used to learn more about elements of an object and what they're composed of. It was found to contain iron, nickel and cobalt; all materials found in chunks of space rocks.

1620. A Yoctosecond is one-trillionth of a trillionth of a second and is comparable to the time that it takes light to cross an atomic nucleus.

1621. There is such a thing as "braille tattoos". They're not like normal tattoos in that they're not made of ink, but instead are made of metal beads that are put under the skin to create designs of braille messages.

1622. The smallest crocodile in the world is the dwarf crocodile. It grows to 1.7 meters in length and weighs only six kilograms.

1623. Shakespeare used about 17,677 words in his plays, sonnets, and narrative poems. He invented about 1,700 or nearly 10% of those words by simply changing the prefixes and suffixes, connecting words together, borrowing from a different language, or simply inventing them altogether.

1624. Former child rock stars Hanson have released a beer called 'Mmmhops'.

1625. The result of a 40-year-long study published in Developmental Psychology points to a correlation between childhood defiance and success later in life.

1626. Most of Wikipedia's entries are written by 1,400 individuals who do little, but contribute to the site, and over 50% of the edits are done by only 524 users.

1627. The KGB once tried to blackmail the then Indonesian president Achmed Soprano with tapes of him having sex with russian women disguised as flight attendants. Except the president was not upset by being blackmailed and in fact, asked for more copies of the video to show back in his country.

1628. In the 13th century, in order to discover which language humans would speak naturally, Frederick II, Emperor of Germany, placed 50 newborns in the care of nurses who would only feed and bathe the babies but not speak or hold them. The emperor never got his answer because all of the infants died.

1629. The fin whale produces an average of 257 gallons (970 litres) of urine each day.

1630. There's a toilet made by Kohler called the numi that has a heated seat, foot warmers, lights, and Bluetooth technology.

1631. Salt and pepper actually comes in liquid form in space. If astronauts tried to sprinkle regular salt and pepper, it would just float around.

1632. Cheese making artists at Dublin Science Gallery made cheese using bacteria from several artists and scientists that were collected using sterile cotton swabs from various parts of their body including a belly button, a mouth, and even tears.

1633. Grand Banks, Newfoundland, Canada, is the foggiest place in the world with 206 foggy days every year.

1634. The California condor is the largest flying bird in North America. Its wingspan can be as wide as 10 feet (3 meters) from tip to tip, and they can fly as high as 15000 feet (4600 meters) if the in the air by catching air currents.

1635. The duck billed platypus and the echidna are the only two mammals to lay eggs.

1636. More twins are born in Nigeria than any other place on earth.

1637. The landscape arch in Arches National Park, Utah, has the longest natural rock span in the world, spanning 290 feet (88 meters).

1638. The peacock spider does a little mating dance to attract a partner. Each type of peacock spider has its own style of dance.

1639. Elephant Island, located off the coast of Antarctica has elephant moss growing on it that is over 5500 years old.

1640. The Nile crocodile rolls and squeezes her eggs in her mouth to help her hatchlings emerge.

1641. The White House, the Empire State Building, the Sears Building, and Dodger Stadium are so large that they have their own zip codes.

1642. There are over 10 million weddings in China every year. Couples spend an average of $12,000 on each, and it's estimated that the wedding industry there will reach $120 billion by 2020.

1643. A service dog named Opal not only leads her blind owner around; she's also become a guide dog to the family's previous guide dog, Edward. The previous dog had taken care of the owner for six years until he had his eyes removed after developing cataracts.

1644. In the original book The Wizard of Oz, Dorothy's magical slippers were actually silver. They were changed to ruby red for the technicolor movie because it was believed that they'd stand out better against the yellow brick road.

1645. Angela Stogner of the University of Vienna Austria discovered that giraffes can hum. The hum is a low frequency sound at about 92 hertz.

1646. There's a restaurant called "Subsix" located at the Per Aquum Niyama Restaurant in the Maldives that is located 20 feet below the surface of the Indian Ocean. You can sit near floor to ceiling glass windows and watch schools of fish and more than 90 coral reef species while you eat.

1647. The Dwarf lantern shark, according to the Guinness Book of World Records, is the world's tiniest shark. Male measures only about 6.3 inches in length.

1648. There's a phenomenon known as "heteropaternal" superfecundation that is so rare that there are only a handful of documented cases in the world. The phenomenon is when two twins have two different fathers.

1649. The gadget was the first atomic bomb ever made and was tested at Trinity Site, New Mexico on July 16th, 1945. The test code named Trinity was a success, unleashing an explosion with the energy of about 20 kilotons of TNT.

1650. Punt guns is a type of gun that was first used in the 1800s. They were used in commercial waterfowl hunting and these guns fired almost one pound shots that could kill 50 to 100 birds in a single shot. The barrels had opening upwards of two inches in diameter and weighed over 99 pounds (44 kg) and measured almost 10 feet (3 meters) long.

1651. One of the richest men of all time, J. Paul Getty, an oil and gas tycoon had a pay phone installed in his house after visitors racked up his phone bill.

1652. The Bohemian Grove is a 137 year-old secret exclusive camp, only open to the rich and powerful men of the world. Richard Nixon was once a member, but cheerfully referred to it as "the most faggy goddamn thing you'll ever imagine."

1653. There's a phenomenon called "Crown Shyness" where in some tree species, their crowns, when fully grown, don't touch each other. The tree canopy ends up with channel-like gaps and the weirdest thing is that scientists aren't sure why it happens.

1654. In the 1996 movie Twister, a recording of a camel's moan was slowed down and used as the sound for the tornado.

1655. Scorpions can survive being frozen and thawed and extreme heat up to 122 degrees Fahrenheit (50 degrees celsius).

1656. Tulips used to be the most expensive flower. In the 1600s, tulips were more valuable than most people's homes and cost almost 10 times what the average working man would earn in a year.

1657. On January 1st, 1976, the day that relaxed marijuana laws came into effect in California, Danny Finegood, an art student at Cal State Northridge, and some of his friends took $50 worth of fabric to the Hollywood sign and changed it to read "Hollyweed". They used the gag as a school project, earning them an A.

1658. In 2002, O.J. Simpson was charged and fined $65 for creating a wake in a manatee zone in his boat in a bay in Florida. He decided to plead innocent instead of paying the fine.

1659. The island on the TV show Gilligan's Island was created in Hollywood in the middle of an artificial lake in CBS's studios. The set cost $75,000 to construct and had artificial palm trees mixed in with real plants and flowers.

1660. When howling together, no two wolves will howl on the same note. Instead, they actually harmonize to create the illusion that there are more of them than there actually are.

1661. The consumption of poppy seeds can actually cause positive results on drug screening tests.

1662. The Darwin's bark spider is small and inconspicuous, but it can spin a web 25 meters across that's able to span an entire river and it's stronger than Kevlar.

1663. In the Miombo Woodland area of Central Africa, scientists discovered an abandoned termite mound that is more than 2,200 years old.

1664. According to the Guinness World Records, the smallest dog in terms of length is Brandy, a female Chihuahua from Florida. She measures only 6 inches (15.2 centimeters) from the nose to the tip of her tail as of January 31st, 2005.

1665. The most lightning-prone place in the world according to NASA is Lake Maracaibo in Venezuela. Storms light up the skies almost 300 nights each year.

1666. The holes at the top of pen caps are there to prevent you from choking if swallowed.

1667. Scientists in Sweden have developed transparent wood that can actually be used as windows.

1668. The restaurant Chomp Eatery in Los Angeles is offering a rainbow grilled cheese sandwich. In fact, the blue tastes like lavender, the green like basil, the red like tomatoes, and the yellow tastes like plain cheese.

1669. According to research done in 2012, published in the journal of Chemosensory Perception, people who scored high on a test for psychopathy had more problems being able to tell different smells apart, and also identifying smells.

1670. San Francisco is the first major U.S. city to require that all new buildings have solar panels installed on the roof.

1671. According to a study done by The University of New South Wales, good manners go a long way. The study found that going out of your way to say thank you makes people see you as a person with greater interpersonal warmth. It can also make you a happier person.

1672. The world's oldest lighthouse is the Tower of Hercules in Spain. It was erected in the first century and is still operational.

1673. Pakistan's parliament is the first parliament in the world to be completely powered by solar energy.

1674. President Calvin Coolidge had a pet raccoon named Rebecca. She was originally supposed to be eaten at their 1926 White House Thanksgiving dinner, but the Coolidge family found her to be friendly and docile and decided to keep her as a pet instead.

1675. It's possible to be allergic to the cold. This allergy, called "cold urticaria", is an allergic response to cold temperatures triggering hives, swelling and itching and if the allergy is severe enough, it can actually result in fainting, shock, or even death and there is no cure.

1676. In a new study published in the Journal of Entomology, a research team from the University of Florida and Union College found that bed bugs love the colors black and red and hate yellow and green.

1677. Evel Knievel, the pioneer of motorcycle long jumping exhibitions, suffered 433 fractured bones and holds the world record for the most bones broken in a lifetime.

1678. The world's largest species of earthworm can be found in Gippsland in southeastern Australia. The giant Gippsland can get as big as 10 feet (3 meters) long.

1679. In 1972, a few years after being elected to Congress, Shirley Chisholm became the first black woman to run for the presidency. She never expected to win, but she ran to prove that Americans could vote for a black woman.

1680. Queen termites have a really long lifespan and they are the oldest termite in the colony. They can live up to 50 years long and produce eggs for up to 10 years.

1681. Melba toast and Peach Melba are both named after the most famous opera singer of the late Victorian era, Dame Nellie Melba.

1682. According to researchers at the Washington University School of Medicine in St. Louis, moms who are supportive and nurturing during their children's preschool years can actually boost the growth of their kids' brains. They found that kids who were nurtured in their early years had a larger hippocampus, the part of the brain tied to learning, memory, and emotion control.

1683. Tokyo has the world's first hedgehog cafe. It has 20 to 30 friendly hedgehogs of different breeds that you can actually spend time with and even take home.

1684. Ukrainian drivers are converting their cars into being fueled by wood burners to save money on expensive gasoline.

1685. Oklahoma man Paul Phillips loves fishing so much that he actually dug up his own pond and then built a house over it. There's a trap door in his living room that he can fish from whenever he wants.

1686. The Japanese spider crab has the largest leg span of any Arthropod, reaching over 12 feet (3.6 meters) in length.

1687. For months, after returning from trips to space, many astronauts report letting go of objects in mid-air, still fully expecting them to float.

1688. Margaret Anne Cargill left all of her stocks to be split between two charities after her death, totaling six billion dollars. This made her the most generous philanthropist in the world in 2012, even though she died in 2006.

1689. Robert Gleason Jr was a convicted murderer who vowed to continue killing his fellow inmates until he was given the death penalty. He finally got his wish in 2013.

1690. John Shepherd-Barron the inventor of the ATM originally intended them to have PINs that were six digits long, but his wife could only remember four digits at a time, so that became the standard.

1691. In 2009 the Nigerian police force arrested a goat on suspicion of attempted armed robbery.

1692. In Russia there's a capsule that's used to treat alcoholism that's implanted under the skin and causes a chemical reaction resulting in shortness of breath, nausea, and mental confusion if the person drinks alcohol. On an unrelated note, about 25% of Russian men die before they hit the age of 55, mostly due to alcohol.

1693. The Kuru-Kuru Nabe is a pot developed in Japan that can stir its own contents when the water inside the pot gets hot enough.

1694. Vin Diesel got his first acting break when he was only 7 years old when he and his friends broke into a theater to vandalize it. A woman stopped them however and offered them a script and 20 dollars each on the condition that they'd attend rehearsal everyday after school.

1695. Ruth Lawrence is a child prodigy who passed the Oxford University Entrance Exam when she was only 10, coming first out of 530 candidates. She graduated after only two years in the bachelor's degree program and she earned a doctorate degree by the time she was 17 years old.

1696. You can actually take a ride on the Hogwarts Express! It's a real train in Scotland called The Jacobite, and has been named for the most beautiful railway route in the U.K.

1697. Male kangaroos flex their biceps and wrestle other males to attract female kangaroos.

1698. Since 2005 Utah has reduced its rate of homelessness by 78% by providing homeless people with apartments and social workers, which actually cost less than the annual ER visits and jail stays.

1699. Finland has the highest rate of recycled bottles in the world. With a return rate of over 90% for plastic bottles and cans and almost 100% for glass bottles.

1700. Danny Lloyd, the actor who played the creepy little kid in 'The Shining', stopped acting as he grew up and went on to become a professor, teaching biology in Louisville.

1701. The Anglo-Zanzibar War lasted only 38 minutes, making it the shortest war in history.

1702. The word 'tsunami' means "harbor wave" in Japanese.

1703. The scent of freshly-mowed grass is the lawn actually trying to save itself from injury. Plants release a number of volatile organic compounds called green leaf volatiles. When plants are injured, these emissions increase like crazy.

1704. The still-beating hearts of live cobras are eaten as a delicacy in Vietnam.

1705. Sea otters have skin pockets where they keep their favorite rocks to keep for cracking open mollusks and clams.

1706. The praying mantis can actually camouflage itself by changing color. It can vary from dark brown to green to blend in with tree bark and leaves. This enables it to hide from predators and also sneak up on prey.

1707. Steven Spielberg named the shark prop used in the 1975 movie Jaws "Bruce" after his lawyer.

1708. Back in the 1920s, there were beach police that actually went around measuring women's swimsuit lengths to ensure that no one was wearing a swimsuit with a questionable length. If a woman was found violating the code, they would be forced to cover up or sent home or, in some cases, actually arrested.

1709. Research from the Chinese Academy of Medical Sciences shows that people who ate spicy foods six to seven times per week had a 14% lower risk of premature death for all causes, rather than people who ate spicy food less than once a week.

1710. On June 10th, 1986, two and a half year old Michelle Funk from Salt Lake City fell into a creek near her home. When rescuers finally pulled her out of the creek over an hour later, she had no pulse and wasn't breathing. Doctors put her on a heart-lung bypass machine and rewarmed her blood. Unbelievably, when her blood finally warmed to 77 degrees Fahrenheit, she woke up and is still living to this day.

1711. The smallest commercial flight in the world is from the Westray Airport to Papa Westray Airport between two small Orkney Islands north of Scotland. It's only a distance of 1.7 miles and if the wind is ideal, it can take as little as 47 seconds from start to finish.

1712. There's a Burger King in Finland with an in-house sauna. The 10-person sauna can be rented for $285 US for three hours and can be used for birthday parties or work events.

1713. KFC in Hong Kong is offering lickable edible fingernail polish in two different flavors, original and hot and spicy.

1714. Amsterdam has a houseboat that is a sanctuary for rescued cats. It's actually become a tourist attraction that receives about 4,500 visitors a year.

1715. According to the World Health Organization, worldwide, up to 5 million people are bitten by snakes every year. The majority of these occur in Africa and Southeast Asia.

1716. According to the World Health Organization, the number of people with diabetes has risen from 108 million in 1980 to 422 million in 2014.

1717. September 10th, 1977, was the very last time that someone was executed by a guillotine.

1718. Uruguayan architect Rafael Vinoly designed a ring-shaped bridge on Uruguay's southern coast, called the Laguna Garzon Bridge, to encourage people to slow down and take in the view.

1719. There are some turtles, such as the Australian Fitzroy River turtle and the North American Eastern Painted turtle that can breathe through their butts as well as their mouths.

1720. The Vermont Novelty Toaster Corporation introduced the toasted selfie. All you have to do is send it a selfie and they'll print it for you on a selfie toast-producing gadget in just 10 days.

1721. Only female mosquitoes bite humans and animals. Male mosquitoes only feed on flower nectar.

1722. Up until the late 1960s, long-haired male visitors to Disneyland were actually turned away because they didn't meet the unwritten dress code.

1723. Bill Gates received an honorary knighthood from Queen Elizabeth, but because he's American, he cannot use the title, sir.

1724. According to the Guinness World Records, the first human cannonball was a woman named Rosa Zazel Richter in 1877. She was shot at a distance of about 20 feet at Westminster Aquarium in London, England.

1725. Rockefeller Center receives an average of 470,000 visitors on any given weekday, and almost 800,000 during the holiday season. The warehouse scene in Raiders of the Lost Ark was actually a matte painting created by artist, Michael Pangrazio. It took him three months to create, was painted on glass, and the live action shots were actually done through a hole in it.

1726. Robert Behnke, a Wisconsin dairy farmer owns the queen cow of milk production. His cow, Gigi, has produced more milk in one year than any other cow, at 8,700 gallons. That's three times the national average for a dairy cow to produce in a year.

1727. According to Professor Charles P Gerba of The University of Arizona's Department of Soil, Water, and Environmental Science, 20% of office coffee mugs carry fecal bacteria.

1728. In 1952, Albert Einstein was actually offered the presidency of Israel. However, he politely declined the offer.

1729. Mountain Dew is an old slang term for moonshine.

1730. The longest highway in the world is Highway 1 in Australia with a total length of 9000 miles (14,500 kilometers).

1731. When Anglerfish mate, they actually fuse together into a single fish.

1732. Emperor penguins can dive to 1850 feet (565 meters) underwater which is deeper than any other bird and can stay under for over 20 minutes.

1733. Steve Jobs once gave a secretary a brand new Jaguar after she told him that she was late because her car wouldn't start.

1734. While we have leap years, we also have leap seconds. Which are added every few years to adjust to the Earth's speed of rotation.

1735. All swans in England are the legal property of the queen.

1736. Scientific research from the London School of Economics and Political Science in 2010, shows that men who are unfaithful tend to have lower IQs.

1737. All surface water of the Atlantic Ocean is significantly saltier than the Pacific Ocean.

1738. The TV-show 'All in The Family' was the first primetime show to have a sound of a flushing toilet. For much of television's history, it was taboo to even show a bathroom, let alone have any sort of bathroom sound.

1739. Author J.K. Rowling, who wrote the Harry Potter series, also writes crime novels under the name Robert Galbraith. Books that she's published under her fake name include "The Silkworm and Cuckoo's Calling."

1740. WD-40 was invented by Norm Larsen back in 1953. He was attempting to concoct a formula to prevent corrosion, a task that's done by displacing water. WD stands for water displacement, and the 40 is because he finally gained success on his 40th attempt.

1741. The band 'Nickelback' got its name from Mike Kroeger's cashier experience at a Starbucks. Customers would pay $1.50 for a coffee that always only cost $1.45, so he would always have to give them a nickel back.

1742. In 1998, Kevin Warwick, a professor of cybernetics at Reading University became the world's first technical cyborg. He had a radio frequency ID implanted in his arm and could turn on the lights by snapping his fingers.

1743. In ancient Rome, women thought that if you wore leather pouch containing a cat's liver on their left foot during sex that it would prevent pregnancy.

1744. In 2014, the United States Department of Agriculture reported that the average American consumes up to 170 pounds of refined sugar every year.

1745. Pablo Escobar, the infamous colombian drug lord, collected exotic animals for his personal zoo. When his house was raided his hippos were released into the wild and now Colombia has the largest hippo outside of Africa.

1746. Instead of keeping your departed loved one in an urn on the fireplace mantle, now, thanks to the company Bios Urn, you can keep them in the form of a tree. Bios Urn created 'Bios Incube', which is an incubator that monitors and cultivates trees from human ashes in people's homes.

1747. Back in 1994, a man named Tony Cicoria was struck by lightning while standing next to a public telephone, and was resuscitated by a nurse who was waiting to use that phone. Not long after his recovery, he noticed that his head became flooded with music, so he went out and bought a piano, and is now a successful composer and performer.

1748. Dinosaurs often used to swallow large rocks. These rocks stayed in their stomach and helped them grind up food.

1749. Ann Hodges from Alabama is the only confirmed person in history that has ever been hit by a meteorite. On a clear day in November of 1954, she was having a nap on her couch when a softball sized hunk of black rock broke through her ceiling, bounced off a radio, and hit her in the thigh, leaving a pineapple shaped bruise.

1750. On January 21st, 1977, on his first day in office, President Jimmy Carter fulfilled a campaign promise by granting unconditional pardons to hundreds of thousands of men who had evaded the draft during the Vietnam War by fleeing the country or failing to register.

1751. Researchers that were training monkeys to recognize themselves in mirrors found that the first thing that the monkeys did was check out all the places on their bodies that they've never seen before, especially their genitalia area. The researchers found them contorting and spreading their legs in front of the mirror to get a better look at previously unseen corners of their bodies.

1752. In Sweden, blood banks send texts to blood donors to notify them whenever their blood helps save a life.

1753. Spain's national anthem, 'Royal March', has no lyrics.

1754. American company Cabot Guns has made the first gun made almost entirely from a piece of Gibeon meteorite that crashed to Earth approximately 4.5 billion years ago. The meteorite was originally found in Namibia in the 1830s.

1755. Bison may look slow and not very agile, but they can run at 35 miles (56 km) per hour and jump as high as six feet off the ground.

1756. There's a new contact lens invented by Canadian optometrist Dr. Garth Webb that can improve human vision beyond 20/20. The bionic lens replaces the natural lens of the eye in a painless eight-minute procedure. It takes effect in only 10 seconds and enhances eyesight for life.

1757. Research conducted at the University of North Carolina concluded that loving someone and being loved in return makes wounds heal faster, due to the release of oxytocin in the blood.

1758. Bruce Wayne, aka Batman, is part owner of the Daily Planet where Clark Kent, aka Superman, works, so essentially, Batman pays Superman's salary.

1759. In 2003, a Coca-Cola employee was fired because he was drinking Pepsi on the job.

1760. Ryan Gosling and Rachel McAdams hated each other when filming 'The Notebook'. However, after finishing the film, they actually fell in love and dated for four years.

1761. The African Union intends on having a single, continent-wide currency modeled after the Euro. The most popular proposed name for the currency as of right now is the Afro.

1762. In ancient Rome, women tried to dye their hair blond with pigeon dung. In Renaissance Venice, they used horse urine.

1763. The word, 'stewardesses', is the longest word that is typed with only the left hand.

1764. New Zealand doesn't have a single land snake, but it does occasionally get visited by sea snakes.

1765. The California grizzly bear was designated as the official state animal of California in 1953, more than 30 years after the last one was killed. It was also honored on the state flag.

1766. Studying the earwax of a blue whale can tell scientists the story of its life. The technique, described in the proceedings of the National Academy of Sciences, can be used as a tool to understand the whale's hormonal and chemical biography. It can also be a window into how pollutants, long discontinued, can still pervade the environment today.

1767. On October 18, 1963, French scientists launched the first cat into space on a Veronique AGI Sounding rocket number 47. The cat, named Felicette, was successfully retrieved after a parachute descent.

1768. Sweden was the first nation to make it illegal to strike a child as a form of punishment known as corporal punishment back in 1979. Since then, many other countries in Europe have also instituted this ban as well as New Zealand and some countries in Africa and the Americas.

1769. According to the Guinness World Records, the largest chocolate bar, by weight, was created by Thorntons in Alfreton, Derbyshire, U.K., on October 7, 2011. The bar measured 12 feet by 14 feet by one foot thick and weighed a whopping 12,700 pounds (5500 kg).

1770. It's illegal except in extreme circumstances to neuter your dog in Norway. They believe in social neutering and training.

1771. The puffer fish or blowfish has enough toxin in it to kill 30 adult humans, and there is no antidote, but amazingly, the meat of some pufferfish is still considered a delicacy.

1772. None of the members of The Beatles could read music. Music was a discovery process for them and did not involve any books.

1773. Mathematician Katherine Johnson is known as the 'computer'. Her obsession with counting allowed her to skip ahead in high school at the age of 10, and in 1961, she calculated the trajectory of NASA's first trip into space and was correct.

1774. The only domestic animal not mentioned in the Bible is the cat.

1775. Nicholas Cage once woke up to a naked man wearing a leather jacket eating a Fudgesicle in front of his bed. After that, Cage could no longer live in that house and moved to the Bahamas.

1776. A man with a Liverpool FC tattoo with the club motto "You'll never walk alone" had his lower leg amputated after a combat injury in Afghanistan. Unbelievably, the surgeon unknowingly cut his tattoo so it now reads "You'll never walk". However, in reality, luckily, the man now has a prosthetic leg and competes in marathons.

1777. The indigenous Sami people of Norway have a tradition of castrating reindeer with their teeth.

1778. Military commandos in Lebanon eat live snakes, a tradition that displays their strength and daring.

1779. Thousands of condoms were issued to soldiers for D-Day. Most of them were used to keep their rifles dry.

1780. Snow monkeys in Japan entertain themselves by making snowballs.

1781. Russian criminals used to get tattoos bearing the images of Lenin and Stalin because it was a commonly held belief that Communist firing squads were not permitted to shoot at an image of their leaders.

1782. Gabe Belfiore of Cortez, Colorado built the 'Dog Gone' vacuum truck. It's used to suck prairie dogs out of their burrows.

1783. Scientists estimate that a single ragweed plant can release one-billion grains of pollen over the course of a single season and can travel hundreds of miles on a gentle breeze.

1784. The great white shark is an example of an apex predator, which means, as an adult, it has no natural predators in its ecosystem.

1785. The pope has his own vehicle that he uses at public appearances called the popemobile. It has bulletproof glass that surrounds him, as well as a handrail for him to hold on to while he stands and waves at the crowd in order to get in and out. It's designed to protect him and still allow him to be visible to the crowds.

1786. Every year, London holds the Great British Duck Race, where people purchase rubber ducks to help support various charities. The ducks are raced more than half a mile down the River Thames, and the first one over the finish line wins a cash prize.

1787. In 2009, they set a world record for the largest plastic duck race with over 205,000 ducks.

1788. The vampire fish impales their prey with their long, sharp fangs. Their fangs can grow as long as six inches.

1789. All NHL hockey pucks are frozen before the game because they glide smoother and faster when frozen.

1790. The trap-jaw ant from Central and South Africa can snap its jaws shut at a speed of up to 145 miles (233 km) per hour. To put that into context, that's 2300 faster than the blink of an eye.

1791. According to a study led by Igor Malyshev, a zoologist at St. Petersburg State University in Russia, the Australian red kangaroo and the eastern gray kangaroos are almost always left handed.

1792. Bellandur Lake in Bangalore, India, is so toxic that it's covered in froth and sometimes bursts into flames. The foam on it is the result of toxic water which has a high amount of ammonia and phosphate, and very low dissolved oxygen because of decades of untreated chemical waste going into it. Because of the amount of grease, oil, and detergent in the froth, it often catches fire.

1793. According to researchers at the Donald O. Perelman Department of Dermatology at The New York University School of Medicine, the higher up you are in altitude, the higher your risk of getting sunburned, and it's quite a bit more, approximately 60% higher.

1794. During the opening ceremony of the Olympic Games, the procession is always led by the Greek team, followed by the other teams in alphabetical order, and the last team is always the team of the hosting country.

1795. There's an isopod called the Cymothoa Exigua that eats fish tongues and then becomes the fish's tongue.

1796. Researchers at McGill University in Montreal, Canada raised a fish called the Polypterus. It can breathe air and walk on land using its front fins.

1797. When lobsters fight or flirt with each other, they actually squirt urine at each other's faces from little urine release nozzles under their eyes.

1798. In 2006, the Hao Sheng Hospital in Japan decorated their maternity ward with all Hello Kitty-themed murals and items to help calm anxious mothers. The cartoon image is on everything, from walls to newborn baby blankets. A giant Hello Kitty figure is dressed in a pink doctor's uniform that even greets visitors in the lobby.

1799. Teratoma tumors can grow hair, teeth, organs, and limbs, and scientists have no idea why they form.

1800. The average person blinks about 12 times per minute. That's about 10,000 blinks on average, per day.

1801. A kitchen faucet would need to be turned on all the way for at least 45 years to equal the amount of blood pumped by the heart in the average lifetime.

1802. The University of Southern Queensland found that facial hair can block up to 95% of the sun's harmful UV rays.

1803. An ostrich' powerful long legs can cover ten to sixteen feet (three to five meters) in a single stride. Their legs can also be formidable weapons. In fact an ostrich kick can kill a human or a potential predator like a lion.

1804. The deepest lake in the world is Lake Baikal in Siberia. It's over 5383 feet (1,641 meters) deep, and is also the most voluminous freshwater lake on Earth, containing nearly 20% of the world's unfrozen fresh water.

1805. On October 2nd, 1954, Elvis Presley made his first and last Grand Ole Opry appearance. Apparently, his gyration-filled performance was not received well and one of the officials there reportedly told him to not quit his day job, which was driving trucks.

1806. Actor Brad Pitt's first acting job was playing a chicken. He wore a chicken suit to attract customers to an El Pollo Loco restaurant in Hollywood. Today, the 55-year-old actor has been in more than 70 movies, won an Academy Award out of five nominations, and more.

1807. While editing his biggest movie, the Titanic, director James Cameron taped a razor blade to the side of the computer with instructions that says, "Use only if the film sucks." But he didn't need to worry very much because the film went on to gross a total of $1.84 billion worldwide.

1808. An underground fire in the coal mines beneath Centralia, Pennsylvania, has been burning since 1962. Astonishingly, nobody knows how the fire even started, but one theory is that burning trash from a nearby landfill accidentally ignited coal beneath the old entrance to the mine. From there, the fire spread wildly through all the mines.

1809. There is a scented cup that tricks your brain into thinking that regular water is actually flavored with citrus, apples, berries, peaches, or cola. The invention, called The Right Cup, was launched on Indiegogo in early 2016 in hopes that people will drink more water if it has a more exciting taste.

1810. The word canvas was derived from the Latin word 'cannabis'. Canvas made from hemp was quite popular among artists who needed a cheap writing material, right up until the end of the 18th century.

1811. Boa constrictors have an innate ability to sense its prey's heartbeat. If it senses a heartbeat, the snake will actually add more pressure until it feels no heartbeat.

1812. There is a humpback whale that has been tracked by Greenpeace since 2008 called Mr. Splashy Pants.

1813. About half of Australia's koalas have chlamydia. In fact, their strain of Koala chlamydia can also infect humans.

1814. You can pay to go on expeditions with National Geographic to exotic places like Antarctica.

1815. There's a golf course in Brisbane, Australia with full grown bull sharks living in the water hazards.

1816. The Pineberry is a white strawberry that tastes like a pineapple.

1817. A study published in the Journal of Neuroscience found that anxiety disengages the prefrontal cortex, a region of the brain that plays an important role in flexible decision making.

1818. The Japanese company YKK makes approximately half of the world's zippers.

1819. Tug of War was once an Olympic sport in the early 1900s.

1820. Two of the world's largest rivers, the Amazon, and the Rio Negro, meet but do not mix and are visually distinct but occupy the same body of water. This is due to the river's different speeds, density, and temperatures.

1821. Research shows that others see you as 20% more attractive than you think you are. This is because when you look in a mirror, all that's reflected are your looks, not your personality.

1822. The world mortgage is derived from French, meaning death pledge. Referring, of course, to the death of a loan because you amortize a mortgage.

1823. It is theoretically possible to get addicted to cuddling. Couples that cuddle a lot can actually experience oxytocin withdrawal when they are apart from each other.

1824. Dogs don't feel guilt or shame. However, they do feel sadness when their owners yell at them.

1825. In Japan's Brazilian Washuzan Highland Park, there's a scary roller coaster called the Sky Cycle. On it, people actually pedal to propel themselves forward through the track.

1826. It is easier to get into Harvard than it is to get a job at Apple's newest store in New York. Harvard's acceptance rate is 7%, while Apple's is only 2%.

1827. In 1979 a woman named Elvita Adams attempted suicide by jumping off the 86th floor of the Empire State Building. She survived when a gust of wind blew her back onto a ledge on the 85th floor.

1828. Pike County farmer and loyal democrat, Valentine Tapley, vowed to never trim his beard again if Abraham Lincoln was elected president in 1860, and he kept his word. His beard grew to 12.5 feet (3.8 meters) long.

1829. In 1964, a pair of Australian scientists, Isabel Joy Bear and RG Thomas, did a study to determine what causes that powerful, wonderful scent of fresh rain.

1830. They determined that it's a mixture of plant oils that are secreted by some plants after an arid period, bacterial spores, and ozone.

1831. On March 29th, 1867, The United States bought 586,412 square miles of land at the northwestern tip of the North American continent, which is the current state of Alaska from Russia. They paid 7.2-million dollars, which amounted to about two cents per acre.

1832. Disney Parks can actually refuse you access to their parks if they find that you have an objectionable tattoo.

1833. Cats can actually get something called whisker stress from eating or drinking out of a bowl that's too small. Whiskers are very sensitive to pressure, and any time they come close to something, it triggers a sensation in your cat. If you see your cat trying to scoop out food with their paw, it might mean that they have whisker stress.

1834. If you consumed coconut oil or coconut meat lately, there's a reasonable chance that it was imported from Thailand. Thailand has been raising and training pig-tailed macaques to pick coconuts for around 400 years. In fact, a male monkey can collect an average of 1,600 coconuts a day and a female can get around 600. A human can only collect around 80 maximum a day.

1835. Narwhal skin is an important source of Vitamin C for the Inuit people. Ounce for ounce, there is almost as much Vitamin C in Narwhal skin as than there is in an orange.

1836. Our urge to breathe is not because of our need for oxygen but our bodies wanting to get rid of carbon dioxide.

1837. David Hasselhoff has a 14 foot (4.27 meter) tall replica of himself from the SpongeBob Squarepants movie.
1838. Cockroaches are not the toughest insect when it comes to resisting nuclear radiation. Insects like the flower beetle have been proven to have higher nuclear radiation resistance.
1839. People who live in Estonia have been able to vote via the internet since 2005.
1840. It has actually snowed in the Sahara desert, in 1979 and 2012.
1841. The trombone was originally called the sackbut.
1842. Port Lincoln, Australia holds an annual festival called the Tunarama. The main event is the world championship tuna toss competition where the winner is the one who can throw their tuna the farthest.
1843. There is a sauna in Norway that can house 150 people. It's a large timber construction set on a beach overlooking the Arctic Ocean.
1844. The bowhead whale, which lives exclusively in the Arctic, has the thickest blubber of all whales. It can get as thick as 28 inches (71 cm).
1845. Hurricane Patricia, from 2015, is the strongest hurricane recorded in the Western Hemisphere. It had winds as high as 200 miles (321 km) per hour.
1846. Owls are unable to roll or move their eyes, so they have to turn their heads to look sideways.
1847. Australians are the world's biggest meat eaters. They consume about 200 pounds (90 kg) per year, and the United States is right behind them, consuming just under that at 198 pounds (89 kg) a year.
1848. According to a study published in the South African Journal of Science, traces of cannabis were detected on pipes that were found in William Shakespeare's garden. Scientists examined 24 pipes using advanced gas chromatography methods and found cannabis on eight fragments, four of which were confirmed from the Bard's garden.

1849. There are little tiny holes or pores in chicken and other bird eggs that allow baby birds to breathe in oxygen and get rid of carbon dioxide. A chicken egg has more than 7,000 pores.

1850. Prince Charles is actually a descendant of Vlad the Impaler, the cruel 15th century Romanian warlord who helped inspire Bram Stoker's 1897 vampire novel, Dracula.

1851. In the 1940s, there was a remote control for the Ga rod TV set that was attached to the set with a 20-foot cable. When you pushed the button.

1852. There's an animal called a wholphin, which is a cross between a false killer whale and bottlenose dolphin. They are hybrids that are believed to live in the wild but have also been born in captivity.

1853. The Nazis had a plot to kill Sir Winston Churchill with a bar of exploding chocolate during the Second World War. Hitler's bomb makers coated explosive devices with a thin layer of dark chocolate and packaged it in expensive-looking black and gold paper, but luckily, the plot was foiled by British spies.

1854. Henry Ford's estimated net worth would have been 200 billion dollars today if he were still alive.

1855. Super Mario was originally known as "Jumpman".

1856. The sea anemone looks like a beautiful flower, but it is really a sea creature that uses venom-laden tentacles to stab passing victims with paralyzing neurotoxin, rendering them helpless.

1857. The word 'prolly', the informal pronunciation of probably originated in the 1940s.

1858. Unlike other planets that take their names from Greek mythology, Uranus' moons are named after characters in Shakespeare's plays. These include Umbriel, Cordelia, and Ariel.

1859. In rural China, hiring strippers to perform at funerals was a common practice in order to attract mourners. It wasn't until 2015 that it was finally banned.

1860. Thousands of microscopic mites live on your face right now. There are two species, Demodex Folliculorum that reside in your pores and hair follicles and D. Brevis that settle deeper in the oily sebaceous glands in your face.

1861. An average elephant can hold and store four liters of water in its trunk.

1862. Large dogs age faster and die younger than small dogs and scientists are still uncertain why this is.

1863. According to vet doctor Joyce Armen, horses can safely drink alcohol because of their huge mass.

1864. Mickey Mouse has a brand recognition of 97% which is higher than Santa Claus.

1865. Spain offers citizenship to the descendants of those who came to the Americas to flee the Inquisition.

1866. There is a reverse color blindness test that exists, where only people who are colorblind can see what the hidden image is.

1867. On April 14th, 1986, Bangladesh was hit by the biggest hailstones ever recorded, weighing in at over 1 kilogram each, killing 92 people.

1868. Before mating, the female giraffe will urinate in the male's mouth. From the taste of her urine, the male can determine if she's in heat or not.

1869. The original Twinkie filling was actually banana-flavored. It wasn't until World War II that there was a banana shortage when vanilla became the standard flavor.

1870. One in two million lobsters is blue; but one in every three million can be yellowy-orange; and even rarer are white lobsters. Each of these colors only shows up about once every few years.

1871. It is possible to cry in outer space. However, your tears never fall; they just sort of sit there like a blob under your eye.

1872. In 2009, in the jungle of the Philippines, scientists discovered a new species of pitcher plant. It's the largest carnivorous plant ever discovered. It's called the "se-Nepenthes attenboroughii", named after Sir David Attenborough. Other meat-eating plants eat things like insects and spiders, but this one's so big that it actually eats rats.

1873. McDonald's Hamburger University trains students in restaurant management skills, and has over 275,000 graduates with a selection rate of one percent at its Shanghai Campus; this intense week-long training program is more exclusive than Harvard.

1874. After years of campaigning by conservationists, in May of 2016, President Obama signed a National Bison Legacy Act into law, making the North American bison the official mammal of the United States. It's the first official mammal recognized by the federal government.

1875. On May 15th, 1809, Connecticut woman Mary Kies was the first American woman to receive a patent. Her innovation was to make a hat by weaving silk or thread into straw, creating a pleasing appearance that became a fashion fad.

1876. The Pacu fish, native to South America, was found in New Jersey in June of 2015. It's a relative of the flesh-eating piranha and is known for its distinctive teeth, which bear an eerie resemblance to human teeth. Luckily, the Pacu fish is not going to bite your face off because it primarily eats plants and is considered mostly harmless to humans.

1877. United Kingdom-based horticulture company Thompson & Morgan has developed a plant that grows both cherry tomatoes and potatoes. It was developed in Canada and is being called the ketchup and fries plant and can be bought in Canadian Costco retailers and even in some independent garden centers.

1878. Some children in southwest China between the ages of 6 and 15 have to scale a cliff about 2600 feet (800 meters) high multiple times a month in order to get to their school. The school, located in Atule'er village, takes about 90 minutes to get to.

1879. At the 2008 Olympics in Beijing, China, visitors could buy seahorse kebabs and deep-fried scorpion. It's estimated that up to 40,000 restaurants ended up adding crazy twist menu items such as this.

1880. Ellen Church was the first female flight attendant who began flying in 1930. She implemented a plan that required all flight attendants to be a registered nurse, which was a great idea, except when World War II began, all of the nurses enlisted in the war, so most airlines were forced to drop the requirement in order to find any workers.

1881. The esophagus of a leatherback sea turtle is lined with papillae, sharp prongs that enable the turtle to dine on jellyfish.

1882. In 2011, Tom Pearcy, a farmer from York, England, created a maze by carving two football-field sized portraits of Harry Potter into a corn field.

1883. If you have an irrational fear of being near, among or in the company of teenagers, you have what's called ephebiphobia.

1884. In ancient Egypt, people were paid for their services in bread and beer. They were also paid in grain, meat and cloth rations, which were considered the necessities of life. But bread and beer were the most basic of the Egyptian diet.

1885. In 2016, the Ed Rolf family from Turkey got food poisoning from eating food that was prepared to celebrate getting out of the hospital for food poisoning.

1886. Ancient Greeks valued political participation and collective governance. The term idiot was used in Ancient Greece to describe someone who did not contribute to politics or the community.

1887. The state of Alaska has over three million lakes. In fact, 86,000 square miles (222,000 square kilometers) of Alaska are covered by water.

1888. Hawks have vision that's about eight times more accurate than humans. They have up to one million photoreceptors in the retina compared to only 200,000 in humans.

1889. The first garbage disposal was invented by architect John W. Hammers in 1927. He wanted to make cleaning up of the kitchen easier for his wife.

1890. In Fairbanks, Alaska, the Aurora Borealis can be seen an average of 240 nights a year. On those nights, the sky is lit up with colors ranging from yellow and greens to reds, purples and blues.

1891. The black and white patterned undersides of a humpback whale are distinctive for each whale. The shape and color patterns on their dorsal fins and flukes are like fingerprints for humans.

1892. In 2013, Navy Veteran Lonnie Bedwell became the first completely blind kayaker to paddle the entire length of the Grand Canyon, 226 miles (363 km) in a solo kayak. It took him 16 days.

1893. There are numbers on the lampposts in New York City's Central Park to help people navigate where they are if they get lost. The first two or three numbers indicate the closest cross street, and the last number indicates what side of town that you're closest to. If you're an odd number, that means you're on the west side, and if you have an even number, that means you're on the east.

1894. There's a beaver dam located in Wood Buffalo National Park in northern Alberta, Canada, that is so large, it can be seen from outer space. It spans 2,789 feet (850 meters) across.

1895. Personal finance website Finder.com has launched a programmable handbag designed to help you monitor and curb your impulsive spending. Using GPS tracking, it can be programmed to lock if you enter your pre-programmed danger zones. It will actually vibrate and flash lights to indicate how many times you've taken out your wallet. It will also flash yellow lights and vibrate every two hours to remind you to put on sunscreen.

1896. In August of 2016, 323 reindeer were killed with a single lightning strike in the Hardangervidda National Park in Norway. They were huddled together because of a heavy storm and were killed because of ground current that had stopped all of their hearts.

1897. A man named Mbah Gotho of Indonesia claims to be 146 years old, and there is a photo of his government ID card to prove it. The card shows his birth date as December 31, 1870. He has outlived all 10 of his siblings, four wives and his children.

1898. The Lithuania village of Ramygala holds an annual beauty pageant where the contestants are goats. Around 500 people brave the summer heat to attend the parade in honor of the goat, a traditional symbol of the northern village.

1899. According to a survey done by Pew Research in 2016, of 1,520 adults living in all 50 states and the District of Columbia, just over one in four people didn't read a single book within the last 12 months.

1900. On May 17th, 2016, a woman named Mary Anne Noland had her obituary published in the Richmond Times which stated that faced with the prospect of voting for either Donald Trump or Hillary Clinton, she literally chose to die.

1901. On May 19th, 2004, a boa constrictor triggered a 15-minute nationwide blackout in Honduras when it got itself trapped between two enormous generation units. The boa was electrocuted and the resulting short circuit caused the emergency system to shut down the entire plant, which shut down the country's electricity.

1902. Rhinotillexomania is the scientific word for picking your nose. "Rhino" means "nose", "tillex" means "habitual picking", and "mania" means "rage or fury".

1903. It's actually possible to cause your eyeball to pop out of its socket, known as exophthalmos, by blowing your nose too hard, vomiting, or coughing excessively. The good news is if you're brave enough, you can just pop it back in.

1904. Arachibutyrophobia is the name for the fear of peanut butter sticking to the roof of your mouth.

1905. The children's ring game 'Ring Around the Rosie' refers to the Great Plague of London in 1665. The 'ring around the rosie' refers to the rosy red rash in the shape of a ring that someone with the plague would develop. The 'pocket full of posie' refers to the fact that people filled their pockets and pouches with sweet-smelling herbs or posies because they believe that the disease was transmitted via bad smells and the 'ashes', which refers to the cremation of the dead bodies.

1906. The word 'Exocannibalism' refers to when you eat someone outside your own family or tribe. 'Endocannibalism' is when you eat someone from the same community or tribe.

1907.	Back in 2013, PayPal accidentally put over $92 quadrillion into PR executive Chris Reynolds' account. PayPal admitted their error and offered to donate money to a cause of Reynolds' choice.

1908.	Jessica Cox, born in 1983 in Sierra Vista, Arizona, was born without arms due to a rare birth defect. She ended up being the first pilot ever to fly with no arms.

1909.	There's a museum in Croatia filled with 507 stuffed frogs. 'Froggyland' shows off the work of 20th century Hungarian taxidermist Ferenc Mere, who spent 10 years stuffing and meticulously arranging the frogs.

1910.	The LG in LG Corporation stands for "Lucky-Goldstar", which is its former name and is the abbreviation of the company's tagline, "Life's good."

1911.	There is a giraffe sanctuary in Kenya called "Giraffe Manor". It's also a hotel where guests can hang out with giraffes and feed them from their windows.

1912.	Viagra was originally developed to treat high blood pressure. The fact that it enhances erections was discovered purely by accident.

1913.	Pigs have the ability to be purposefully manipulative. They're intelligent enough to pinpoint a weak spot, remember it, and use it to their advantage later on.

1914.	The 'Free Little Library' is a nonprofit organization that was started back in 2009 that offers free books in many little libraries in communities all over the world. Today, there are over 50,000 book exchanges worldwide.

1915.	Bedbugs don't have wings and they can't fly or jump. They can, however, live for months without food.

1916.	The world's largest snake, an eight-meter-long, approximately 250-kilogram reticulated python, was captured at a Malaysian construction site. The snake ended up dying just three days later after its discovery while laying an egg.

1917. Japan is about to build a 123-meter Ferris wheel and it's going to have see-through floors. The Redhorse Osaka Wheel will be the fifth-tallest Ferris wheel in the world and the tallest in Japan.

1918. Fruitarianism is a subset of veganism. It's a diet that consists primarily of fruit and possible nuts and seeds. In fact, some fruitarians will only eat what falls or what would naturally fall from a plant.

1919. A study published in the journal 'Brain Structure and Function' found that after monitoring mice under the effects of both silence and different types of noise, that two hours of silence per day promoted cell growth in the part of the brain that controls memory, emotion, and learning.

1920. According to the National Institution of Health, one out of every 2,000 to 3,000 babies born is born with teeth. They're called natal teeth.

1921. In Tennessee, a law exists that prohibits the sale of bologna on Sunday.

1922. City birds use cigarette butts to line their nests in order to drive away parasites, as the nicotine in cigarettes acts as a natural pesticide.

1923. Every single president Egypt has ever had has either left the position by being arrested into military custody, or died in office.

1924. There's an animal native to east Asia called the raccoon dog. It looks like a raccoon, but is actually a dog.

1925. The little brown myotis bat can consume up to 1,000 mosquitoes in one hour.

1926. Dolphins actually have two stomachs, one for storing food, and the other for digesting it. Basically, they're water cows, except way smarter and a little prettier. Dinosaur fossils have been found on every major continent in the world. They've been found in Antarctica, Australia and India, and in the far north of Canada. The Goliath frog is the largest frog in the world. It can reach up to 12.5 inches in length and weighs 7.2 pounds (3.27 kg).

1927. On May 31, 2014, according to the Guinness World Records, 104 volunteers at the Deer Run Camping Resort in Gardners,

Pennsylvania, made the largest s'mores ever. It weighed a whopping 267 pounds (121 kg).

1928. Because camels live in conditions where there is little water, their digestive systems wring their food dry of almost all of its moisture. In fact, their poop is so dry, you can actually use it to start a fire.

1929. The Pagoda in Japan is the oldest wooden building in the world. It was built using trees from 600 AD.

1930. The planet Jupiter has a total of 63 moons that have been discovered to date.

1931. Gummy bear candies were originally called dancing bears. Hans Riegel originally created them back in 1920, which were originally made out of licorice.

1932. There's a building near Newark, in Ohio, shaped like a picnic basket. It was built by Dave Longaberger, owner of Longaberger Basket Company in 1997 to be used as his head office.

1933. The United States has had two presidents who were both peanut farmers, Thomas Jefferson and Jimmy Carter.

1934. In Tanzania, almost two out of every five girls get married before they turned 18. That's almost 15 million girls a year.

1935. The hagfish has no jaws, no bones in its body and is able to tie itself into a knot.

1936. In August of 2016, the first documented case of twin dogs were born via C-section at Rant en Dal Animal Hospital in Mogale City, South Africa.

1937. To stay cool in hot temperatures, kangaroos lick their arms until their fur and skin is sopping wet. The wind hitting their arms causes the saliva to evaporate and cool them off.

1938. Movie theaters are forbidden in Saudi Arabia and have been banned since the 1980s.

1939. According to Guinness World Records, Anthony Victor from India has the longest ear hair ever. It measures over seven inches at its longest point.

1940. The Chinese have recorded solar eclipse sightings all the way back since 720 BC.

1941. The Hammetschwand lift in Switzerland is the highest exterior elevator in Europe. It connects a rock path with the lookout point Hammetschwand on a plateau overlooking Lake Lucerne. It takes passengers 502 feet (153 meters) up the summit in less than a minute.

1942. The Slinky was accidentally invented by Richard James. Richard was a naval engineer, and while working with tension springs in 1943, discovered that when one of the springs fell, it kept moving. He thought it would make a great toy, and the Slinky toy was born.

1943. In the 1980s, a musician named Daryl Davis befriended members of the KKK in Maryland, causing them to disband in that state because they learned all about the misconceptions of black people from Davis.

1944. To this day, 4% of the sand on Normandy beaches is made of shrapnel from the original fight on D-Day.

1945. It is illegal in many countries to perform surgical procedures on an octopus without anesthesia due to their intelligence.

1946. Hugh Jackman didn't know that Wolverines were actual animals until he started filming X-Men.

1947. According to the World Health Organization and UNICEF, hand washing with soap is a more effective way to prevent disease than any vaccine out there.

1948. Jason Lewis journeyed around the world between 1994 and 2007 by biking, rollerblading, kayaking, and pedaling and became the first person to circumnavigate the globe by pure human power.

1949. After Seth Rogen released the parody to the Bound 2 music video, Kanye West, actually, invited him to give feedback on every new song off his new album.

1950. According to statistics, most missing children are abducted by relatives and parents.

1951. Shockingly, most energy drinks don't contain as much caffeine as coffee. A Grande coffee at Starbucks has 320 milligrams of caffeine, which is four times the 80 milligrams of caffeine that can be found in an average can of Redbull.

1952. Clint Eastwood was the mayor of Carmel, California, from 1986 to 1988. His salary was $200 a month.

1953. IKEA in Australia once gave away cribs to couples that could prove that their babies were born on November 14th, exactly nine months to the day from Valentine's Day.

1954. There's an umbrella called the "Oombrella" that can actually predict when it's about to rain and send an alert to your smartphone reminding you to bring your umbrella along. Not only that, but if you forget it in a restaurant, it can send you a notification via Bluetooth that you forgot it before you get too far.

1955. Ancient Egyptian pharaohs made slaves fan their wine all night to cool it down.

1956. Jellyfish are the ocean's most efficient swimmers. They consume 48% less oxygen than any other swimming animals.

1957. Scientists from Tufts University have created worms with the heads and brains of other species of worms by manipulating cell communication. Instead of altering their DNA, the scientists manipulated proteins that control conversations between cells.

1958. According to the Guinness World Records, the oldest message in a bottle spent 108 years, four months, and 18 days at sea. It was put in the sea by the Marine Biological Association in the United Kingdom in November of 1906. It washed ashore on Amrum Island in Germany on April 17, 2015.

1959. The Shin-Yokohama Ramen Museum in Yokohama City, Japan, is a museum dedicated to the ramen noodles.

1960. Bees in Ribeauville, France started producing honey in different shades of blue and green. When the beekeepers investigated, they actually found that instead of collecting nectar from flowers, the bees were feeding on remnants of colored M&M candy shells that were being processed by a plant 2.5 miles (4 km) away.

1961. The largest meteorite and largest piece of iron ever found is the Hoba meteorite. It was discovered in 1920 in Namibia, by a farmer who was plowing his field. The meteorite weighs 66 tons and measures 8.9 feet (2.7 meters) long and wide and about 3 feet (1 meter) thick. Experts estimate that it fell to earth about 80,000 years ago.

1962. Cows, sheep and goats all have a tough dental pad below their top instead of front teeth. This dental arrangement helps ruminants gather great quantities of grass and fibrous plants.

1963. When the Krakatoa volcano in Indonesia erupted in 1883, the sound it made could be heard thousands of miles away in Australia and the island of Rodriguez. It was the loudest sound ever recorded on the planet.

1964. The microscopic tardigrade, also known as water bear, or moss piglets, is one of the world's toughest creatures. It can go a decade without water, and can withstand temperatures as low as -459 degrees Fahrenheit (-272 celsius) as well as highs of 304 degrees Fahrenheit (151 celsius).

1965. Adult rats can fit through a hole as small as a quarter, or a gap less than one inch wide. This is how rats can infest your home without your knowledge.

1966. According to researchers at the National Hansen's Disease Program in Baton Rouge, Louisiana, the armadillo is one of the few mammals that harbor the bacteria that causes leprosy.

1967. There is a musical road in Lancaster, California. It was created as a TV ad for Honda. The road is cut into groves that when traveling about 50 miles (80 km) per hour, it will actually play William Tell's Overture.

1968. From 1956 to 1958 Chrysler offered a record player in its new cars called the Highway Hi-Fi. But it was short lived because they had a tendency to break.

1969. Author, American sex therapist, and media personality, Dr. Ruth, was trained as a sniper when she was just 16 years old by the underground Jewish military organization Aganah in Israel.

1970. In 1992, locals from Zernikow, Germany discovered a 100-tree swastika during an aerial survey. The swastika was made up of a group of large trees only visible from the air and was almost 7 square miles (19 square meters). In autumn, the yellowing trees stand out against the surrounding evergreens. Nobody knows who planted these trees, but it is known that it was created during Hitler's peak in the 1930s.

1971. The world's largest pool is in the seaside resort of San Alfonso del Mar in Chile. It was built in 2006 and is 114 feet (35 meters) deep and is filled with 65 million gallons (249 million liters) of water.

1972. Scientists at Duke University have developed a device that allows monkeys to control robotic wheelchairs by sending signals with their brains. They're hoping that one day it will help people with disabilities.

1973. Chiayi, Taiwan, built a 55 foot (17-meter) glass structure shaped like a giant high heel shoe. It's used as a wedding hall and a tourist attraction. It was built in honor of women who suffered from arsenic poisoning from well water that caused gangrene, a condition sometimes known as black foot disease.

1974. 36-year-old Wang Xiaoyu is a Chinese hair stylist trained in the art of kung-fu. He cuts hair while standing on his head.

1975. Not only does the Earth spin on its axis, it also moves around the sun at a speed of about 66,000 miles (107,000) kilometers an hour.

1976. In 1984, Jack Lalanne, sometimes referred to as the 'Godfather of Fitness', towed 70 rowboats with passengers in them from Queensway Bridge to the ship Queen Mary while shackled, handcuffed, and fighting winds and currents.

1977. 'Happy Hour' has been illegal in the Republic of Ireland since 2003 under the Intoxicating Liquor Act.

1978. Rodents are incapable of vomiting. They can't puke because of anatomical constraints. In other words, they simply aren't built with the ability to.

1979. On the Norwegian island of Spitsbergen sitting inside a mountain is the Svalbard Global Seed Vault, which holds over 850,000 copies of seeds from across the planet just in case of a global catastrophe.

1980. A tiger's tongue is so coarse it can actually lick flesh down to the bone.
1981. Bhutan, the world's most eco-friendly country, once planted 108,000 trees to celebrate the birth of its new prince.
1982. A group of bears is called a "sloth of bears."
1983. Steven Tyler estimates that he spent at least five to six million dollars on cocaine in his lifetime.
1984. In the 1950s, psychologist Fredric Wertham wrote a book called "Seduction of the Innocent" that accused Batman and Robin of being homosexual and Superman of being a fascist right-wing fantasy.
1985. When it was first released, there was a lot of debate over the identity of the unknown wizard at the back of the Harry Potter and the Philosopher's Stone first edition. The illustrator, Thomas Taylor, later revealed he based it on his father after being told to draw a wizard to decorate the back cover.
1986. Pigeons actually produce milk to feed their young.
1987. Jackie Chan is the highest paid actor in Asia.
1988. Pablo Escobar used to cheat at Monopoly games with his kids, hiding extra money ahead of time near where he planned to sit.
1989. Amazonian butterflies drink turtle tears in order to receive mineral sodium from them.
1990. When a cat rubs their face on an item, they're not merely scratching themselves; they're actually leaving their own scent behind. Cats have glands located around their mouths, chins, inside of their face, neck and ears. This is called "bunting."
1991. People throw away approximately $4.5 million into fountains and wishing wells every single year.
1992. Big Bang Theory and Two and a Half Men creator Chuck Lorre wrote The Teenage Mutant Ninja Turtles theme song.
1993. Michigan judge Hugh Clarke actually held himself in contempt after his own smartphone rang in court.
1994. A mosquito's proboscis, or nose, has 47 sharp edges on its tip to help cut through skin, and can even cut through protective clothing.

1995. There is a drug called "Truvada", which has been shown to prevent HIV infection at a 92% success rate for gay men, and a 70% success rate for intravenous drug users, but unfortunately less than 1% of at-risk people currently take the drug, and only 1/3 of primary care doctors have even heard of it.

1996. Many Japanese bathrooms have a button that when pushed, plays the flushing sound to mask the sound of your own "business".

1997. In 2015, Croatia launched a program called "Fresh Start" which wiped away debt for 60,000 low income Croatians who had been struggling to pay their bills, in an effort to boost consumer confidence and spending. The state, along with firms and banks, agreed to forgive up to 60,000 Kuna or 8,830 dollars per individual.

1998. According to astronomers at the Australian National University, there are ten times more stars in the night sky than there are grains of sand in the world's deserts and beaches.

1999. Even though the Church of Scientology has been in Germany since 1970, the German government doesn't recognize it as a religion and sees it instead as an abusive business masquerading as a religion.

2000. Alpacas can get sick or even die from loneliness, so it's always best to have them in pairs or more.

2001. About 90% of the world's population lives in the northern hemisphere. This means that only about 700 million people live in the southern hemisphere.

2002. According to biologists working at Newfoundland's Memorial University, bread is junk food for ducks because it makes them fat and disease-ridden.

2003. Dogs watch more TV now than they did before because of flat screen televisions which flicker at a rate that a dog's eyes are actually able to process.

2004. The Bororo people are an indigenous race in Brazil and all share the same blood type. Type O.

2005. Beethoven began losing his hearing at the age of only 28, so he cut the legs off his piano so that he could sit on the floor and compose music by feeling the vibrations of the piano.

2006. The Greater Honeyguide bird guides people to beehives and after the honey is taken out the bird eats what's left of the hive.

2007. After the Second World War, crystal meth was prescribed as a diet aid and remained legal right up until the 1970s.

2008. The Second Chance Coffee Company in Illinois conducts FBI background checks to make sure that those seeking employment in the company have actually been to prison, because the company only hires ex-inmates.

2009. Rabbits eat their own poop every day. They produce special poop called "Cecotropes", or night feces, which are nutrient rich and are passed out of the body like normal stool, but are a little different. They can later be re-ingested by the rabbit safely so that important nutrients can be reabsorbed.

2010. The menstrual pad, when it was first invented, used to be held up by a belt.

2011. A Cornell food and brand lab study of 497 diners showed that patrons who order their dinner from a heavy server ordered significantly more food, were four times more likely to order dessert, and ordered 17% more alcohol.

2012. In November of 2015, Nestle admitted that they used slave labor in the production of its 'Fancy Feast' cat food brand in Thailand.

2013. Coffea charrieriana, discovered in 2008, is the first known coffee plant that contains no caffeine.

2014. Haagen-Dazs ice cream was founded in 1961 by Reuben and Rose Mattus, two Jewish-Polish immigrants, in the Bronx, New York. They invented the Danish sounding name as a tribute to Denmark's exemplary treatment of the Jews during the Second World War, and included an outline map of Denmark on early labels.

2015. In 2002, actor Vin Diesel saved an entire family from a burning car wreck.

2016. The Muppets creator Jim Henson believed in allowing a character to grow organically. His guiding philosophy was that each Muppet had a distinct personality. In fact, he believed that it was the job of the puppeteer to uncover it.

2017. It can take anywhere from 90 to 120 minutes just to hard-boil an ostrich egg.

2018. The saying 'Bless You' after a sneeze comes from the 14th century Pope Gregory VII who asked for it to be said after every sneeze in order for it to protect him against the plague.

2019. Mosquitoes survive the impact of raindrops using a zen-like approach of non-resistance.

2020. The legendary horror writer R.L Stine got his start by writing comics for Bazooka Joe bubble gum under the pen name Jovial Bob Stine.

2021. Nintendo 64 wasn't always called 'Nintendo 64'. It began as Project Reality and then it was renamed to Nintendo Ultra 64 before they finally shortened it to simply Nintendo 64.

2022. Pentheraphobia is the fear of your mother-in-law. The origin of the word 'penthera' is Greek, meaning "mother-in-law", and 'phobia', in Greek, meaning "fear".

2023. The game bingo was originally called "Beano" because players used beans to cover the numbered squares.

2024. The most commonly broken bone is the clavicle, more commonly known as the collarbone.

2025. The first person to ever go over Niagara Falls and survive was 63-year-old schoolteacher Annie Edson Taylor back in 1901.

2026. In 1848, an ice jam up the river from Niagara Falls caused the falls to stay bone-dry for nearly 48 hours. Some people actually took it as a sign that the world was ending and attended special services at local churches. Normally, it has the highest flow rate of any waterfall in the world and provides 4.4 gigawatts of energy to the region.

2027. In 2008, Burger King introduced a new product for the Christmas season called "Flame", meat-scented cologne for meat-loving men. It was promoted as the scent of seduction with a hint of flame-broiled meat.

2028. Newborn giraffes stand at about 6 feet (1.83 meters) tall, making them taller than most humans.

2029. The food coloring known as "carmine" is extracted from the female cochineal insect shells boiled in ammonia or sodium carbonate solution, and it's in more things than you might think. It actually makes ice cream, yogurt, candy, and red fruit drinks.

2030. It's a faux pas in Russia to give your date a dozen roses. You give an odd number of flowers for a happy occasion and an even number for condolences.

2031. Expiration dates for bottled water is actually for the bottle, not for the water in it.

2032. An elephant can actually die of a broken heart if their mate dies. They may refuse to eat or lay down, shedding tears until they starve to death.

2033. There is a species of orchid that only grows at high elevations in certain mountainous areas of Ecuador, Colombia, and Peru, that looks just like a monkey.

2034. According to the National Retail Federation, the four most common grocery items shoplifted are cigarettes, energy drinks, high-end liquor and infant formula.

2035. The farthest flight on a hoverboard was 900 feet (275 meters) and was achieved by Alexandru Duru in Quebec, Canada, on August 25th, 2014.

2036. A U.K. woman named Tess Christian claims that she has not smiled or laughed in 40 years, all in an effort to prevent wrinkles.

2037. On May 8th, 2010, actress Betty White, who was 88 at the time, became the oldest person to host Saturday Night Live.

2038. Indonesian scientists have created a birth control pill for men by using a plant called the gendarussa. It's 99% effective.

2039. The urine from a Maned Wolf smells like marijuana.

2040. Indonesia's Kawah Ijen volcano burns blue along with its lava because of the high amounts of sulfur gas contained within it.

2041. Crocodiles can hold their breath underwater for up to two hours if they need to. The colder the water, the longer that they can stay under because a cold crocodile uses less energy and oxygen than a warm one.
2042. The 1925 released film, Ben Hur, was the most expensive silent film ever made. Costing between four to six million dollars at that time.
2043. Actress Margaret Hamilton, who is most remembered for her scary portrayal of the wicked witch in The Wizard of Oz, and terrifying children everywhere, was actually a kindergarten teacher before she got into acting.
2044. In Spain and France the tooth fairy is a mouse. Known as the la bonne petite souris, the tiny mouse will procure teeth left under pillows replacing them with either cash or sweets.
2045. In 1985, Lynette Woodard became the first woman to play for the Harlem Globetrotters. Since then, she has played in the WNBA and has been inducted into the Basketball Hall of Fame and Women's Basketball Hall of Fame.
2046. If you have delusions where you think you're a wolf or other wild animal, you suffer from what's called lycanthrope.
2047. India has 23 official languages. While Hindi is the official language of the central government in India, with English as a provisional official sub language. Individual state legislatures are free to adopt any regional language as the official language of that state.
2048. There's an annual sidewalk egg frying contest on the Fourth of July in Oatman, Arizona. Contestants are given 15 minutes to fry two eggs using only solar power. They can use mirrors, magnifying glasses, and aluminum to help speed up the process.
2049. Pablo Picasso's full name was, Pablo Diego José Francisco de Paula Juan Nepomuceno Crispín Crispiniano María Remedios de la Santísima Trinidad Ruiz Picasso.
2050. The library of Congress is the largest library in the world. It has more than 162 million items, over 838 miles (1350 km) of bookshelves, more than 38 million books and print materials, 3.6

million recordings, 14 million photos, 5.5 million maps, 7.1 million pieces of sheet music, and 70 million manuscripts.

2051. Baby hedgehogs are born with quills but they are soft and flexible.

2052. In the early days of the Indie 500, most of the cars had two seats. One for the driver and one for the onboard mechanic. The mechanic monitored the gauges, made repairs, and sometimes would even massage the driver's arms and neck. The onboard mechanic was mandatory from 1912 to 1922, and then again from 1930 to 1937.

2053. Boxer and Olympic gold medalist George Foreman has five sons and he named all of them George.

2054. There's a hotline in Germany called "Schimpf-los", which means "swear away", where people can call to let off steam after a stressful day at work.

2055. In 2013, Mark Zuckerberg spent 30 million dollars buying four houses that surround his home, just to make sure that he has privacy.

2056. In 2012, a Swedish man named Peter Skyllberg survived for two months in a snowed in car by eating snow and staying warm in a sleeping bag.

2057. In 1993, a lawyer named Garry Hoy in Toronto decided to show off to a group of law students just how durable his office's windows were by body-checking one. Unfortunately, the window didn't shatter and instead popped out of its frame and he ended up falling 24 stories to his death.

2058. The coldest village on earth is Oymyakon in Russia. The average temperature in January averages negative 123 degrees fahrenheit (51 degrees Celsius), and their all-time low is negative 91 degrees fahrenheit (71 degrees Celsius) in February.

2059. In Crater Lake in central Oregon, there is a floating tree trunk known as the "Old Man of The Lake" that has been bobbing completely vertically in the lake for well over a hundred years. It's been referenced in writing as far back as 1896.

2060. The octopus, squid, and the salmon all die soon after giving birth. For the most part, males die soon after fertilizing the females' eggs, and the females only live long enough to birth their young before dying.

2061. The Amazon rainforest is home to 427 mammals, 1,300 birds, 378 reptiles, and more than 400 amphibians.

2062. Google was originally named "Backrub".

2063. In 2006, an analysis of cat's tongues showed that they do not have the taste receptors that react to sweet-tasting things. Every feline from lions to tigers down to the domestic housecat cannot taste anything sweet.

2064. There's a resort in Finland called Kakslauttanen Arctic Resort, where your accommodations are a glass igloo.

2065. The recessed dip on the facial structure of your skull between your eyes and above the bridge of your nose is called the nay-see-an. Cosmetic surgeons rely heavily on the type of nay-see-an a person has when planning a rhinoplasty, a.k.a. "nose job".

2066. August 13th is officially Left Handers Day.

2067. In some African countries, albinos' body parts are believed to bring wealth and good luck. Disturbingly, as a result, attackers chop off their limbs and pluck out their organs and sell them to witch doctors.

2068. Elephants are now being trained for bio detection in South Africa. They are being tested to see if they can utilize their heightened sense of smell to look for poachers, land mines, and explosives. Elephants have 1,948 genes dedicated to smelling, whereas dogs only have 811 and humans only have just under 400.

2069. In 2006, Evel Knievel sued Kanye West for his video in the song Touch the Sky, in which Kanye takes on the persona of Evel Knievel and jumps a motorcycle over a canyon.

2070. Singer Barry Manilow wrote the 'State Farm like a Good Neighbor' jingle. He was paid a flat fee of $500.

2071. Researchers at Norway's University of Bergen have found a link between being addicted to work and anxiety. They looked at more than 16,000 workers across the country and found that nearly 8% of workaholics were more likely to suffer from ADHD, OCD, depression, and anxiety. They also found that people who work more than 55 hours per week were at a higher risk of heart attack and stroke.

2072. On November 14, 1969, the Apollo 12 was struck by lightning just 36 seconds after liftoff. And moments later, it was struck again. The second strike tore through the ship, and wiped out many of its electrical systems. One of the flight controllers remembered how to switch the spacecrafts signaling conditioning equipment to auxiliary, and the Apollo 12 was able to actually continue onto successfully land on the moon.

2073. Actress Megan Fox suffers from papyrophobia, which is the fear of dry paper.

2074. In the 16th century, up until the 1960's, Egyptian mummies were actually ground and used to produce a brown paint color called Mummy Brown. The powder was mixed with white pitch and myrrh to produce a rich brown pigment.

2075. During the Vietnam War, U.S. Fighter jets would drop their external fuel tanks over Vietnam when they were empty or the pilot needed more maneuverability. Vietnamese farmers would then repurpose them and use them as canoes.

2076. A 68 year old grandmother from West Wales had her car followed and swarmed for two days by 20,000 bees. They were actually trying to rescue their queen bee, which unbeknownst to her, had hitched a ride in her Mitsubishi Outlander. Beekeepers were brought in to safely remove them.

2077. The hood ornament on a Rolls Royce car is actually called the Spirit of Ecstasy.

2078. In 1974, Gerber baby products tried marketing singles by Gerber, which were meals in a jar like creamed beef and beef burgundy. Marketing was aimed to college students and young adults. The product failed!

2079. Believe it or not, Nintendo was originally a playing card company, founded in late 1889. It was based in Kyoto, Japan, and produced and marketed a game called "Hanafuda". In fact, Nintendo continues to manufacture playing cards in Japan and even organizes its own tournament called the Nintendo Cup.

2080. According to a study done in 2002 by Daphne Soares from the University of Maryland, an American alligator can orient themselves to the ripples created by a single drop of water, even in complete darkness. This is because their faces and bodies are covered with tiny bumps that are far more sensitive than our own fingertips.

2081. During the filming of 'Wolf of Wall Street', actor Jonah Hill snorted so much fake cocaine, which was vitamin D powder, he ended up being sick for six weeks with bronchitis.

2082. According to a study done in 2015 by Common Sense Media and CEO James Steyer, the average teen spends up to nine hours a day on social media.

2083. There are actually three different types of tears. Basal tears keep your eyes lubricated. Irritant or reflex tears are produced when you get something in your eye and emotional tears, of course, are produced during moments of intense feeling.

2084. The Mutter Museum in Philadelphia has an exhibit of a woman's body that was naturally converted into soap due to the chemicals in the soil where she was buried.

2085. The average sloth travels only 123 feet (37 meters) per day. That's less than half the length of a football field.

2086. Chewing gum causes increased saliva, which increases swallowing, which increases the amount of air that you swallow, which makes you pass gas more.

2087. Gangsta's Paradise is one of the few Coolio songs to not feature any profanity because it was the only way that Stevie Wonder would authorize the sampling of his song, Pastime Paradise.

2088. Leopards are solitary animals that prefer to hunt and live alone and only get together with other leopards to mate. Also, they can eat things that are twice their size.

2089. The sound of Velociraptors talking back and forth to each other in the movie Jurassic Park was actually the sound of mating tortoises.

2090. The founder of IKEA, Ingvar Feodor Kamprad, started his career at age six, selling matches. At the age of 10, he was going around the neighborhood on his bike, selling Christmas decorations. Then, at the age of 17, he was getting money from selling fish and pencils. Finally, after his father gave him a small sum of money for doing well in school, he started IKEA.

2091. New York City's 9-1-1 systems handle more than 11 million calls per year, making it the largest of its kind in the nation.

2092. There's a religion called Dudeism, based on the movie "The Big Lebowski", which advocates the practice of going with the flow, being cool headed, and taking it easy.

2093. Created in Italy, "Let's Pizza" is the world's first pizza vending machine and can deliver fresh pizza with custom toppings in only three minutes.

2094. Maryana Naumova is a 16 year old Russian powerlifter who can bench press 370 pounds (170 kilograms).

2095. City raccoons are very intelligent and have learned to adapt to their urban environment by opening doors and trash bins.

2096. In 1986 a French woman named Nadine Vaujour was so determined to get her husband out of jail that she learned how to fly a helicopter and flew over the prison where he was at to pick him up off of a roof. And she did! But was arrested shortly after.

2097. The Maruyama Zoo in Japan spent four years trying to mate two hyenas before realizing that they were both male.

2098. In 2014 the Journal of Neuroscience found that brain patterns synchronize when people have conversations, as our brains are constantly trying to predict what the person is trying to say next.

2099. As of July 2015, 600 billion LEGO parts have been produced. Which is about 86 pieces for each person on the planet.

2100. In Thailand people text 555 to each other instead of "hahaha" because the number five is pronounced "ha" in Thai.

2101. The Citarum river in Indonesia is considered the most polluted river in the world. Full of dyes, chemicals, and a lot more nasty stuff.

2102. There was an ancient Chinese custom where girls would have their toes and arches broken, tied, and bound underneath their feet before the arch of the foot could develop. This was done so that their feet could fit into tiny little shoes. Back then, small feet in China represented the height of female refinement.

2103. There is a phobia called "Koumpounophobia" where sufferers have a paralyzing fear of buttons. The specific fear varies from person to person, but some people feel that buttons are dirty and some are afraid of the texture of certain buttons.

2104. A woman named Vesna Vulovic from Yugoslavia holds the Guinness World Record for the highest fall survived without a parachute. On January 26, 1972, she was working as a flight attendant when she fell over 32,000 feet (10,000 meters) over the Czech Republic. Unbelievably, the plane that she was working aboard blew up and she fell inside a section of the tail unit. After being in the hospital for 16 months and emerging from a 27 day coma, she had multiple broken bones but miraculously survived.

2105. Ontario, Canada, has more than 250,000 lakes and contains about one-fifth of the entire world's fresh water.

2106. NASA scientists have discovered that about 4.3 billion years ago, Mars may have had enough water to cover its entire surface in a liquid layer about 137 meters deep. This primitive ocean would've held more water than the Arctic Ocean. However, over time, it lost about 87% of that water into space.

2107. Researchers from the French university, Universite Libre de Bruxelles found that cockroaches have their own personalities and even display different character traits. They are simple animals, but they can make complex decisions on survival, and one cockroach's decision can actually sway anothers.

2108. In 2008, a man named Ian Usher from Perth, Australia, sold his entire life on eBay for $399,000 following the breakdown of his marriage. The sale price included his home, his car, his motorcycle, a two-week trial in his job, and an introduction to his friends.

2109. There's a disorder called "Congenital Amusia" where people can't recognize common songs from their culture, can't tell when notes are out of tune, and sometimes say that music sounds like banging to them.

2110. In ancient Greece, the apple was thrown at someone to symbolically declare one's love for them. This is because in Greek mythology, the Greek goddess Eris became disgruntled after she was excluded from a wedding; and in retaliation, tossed a golden apple inscribed with "For the most beautiful one" into the wedding party. At that point, it was claimed by Aphrodite, and thus became a symbol for love.

2111. According to the World Health Organization, an estimated 350 million people globally suffer from depression. It's also a leading cause of disability worldwide, and is a major contributor to the overall global burden of disease.

2112. Koalas have human like fingerprints; in fact, they're almost identical to human ones. Not even careful analysis under a microscope easily distinguishes the loopy, whorled ridges on koala's fingers from our own.

2113. For five years, a woman named Oxana Malaya from the Ukraine lived with dogs and survived on raw meat and scraps. She walked on all fours, panted with her tongue hanging out, whined, and even barked. After she was abandoned by her alcoholic parents, she was actually raised by a pack of dogs on a run-down farm in the village of Novaya. When she was finally discovered in 1991, she had almost forgotten how to speak.

2114. During the first three years, a child's brain triples in weight and establishes about 1,000 trillion nerve connections.

2115. Road traffic crashes are the leading cause of death among children ages 10 to 19.

2116. Omphalophobia is the fear of the belly button. Sufferers of this are actually afraid to have their belly buttons touched or to touch another persons.

2117. Some baby whales are actually born with hair. Most species born with hair usually lose it over the first several days or weeks of birth.

2118. According to a study done by Nick Wolfinger, a sociologist at the University of Utah, people have a better chance of not getting divorced if they get married between the ages of 28 and 32.

2119. Abu Dhabi has the largest falcon hospital in the world. In fact, it houses over 6,000 falcons.

2120. North Yungas Road in Bolivia has the nickname, "Death Road," because it's estimated that between 200 to 300 people per year die on it.

2121. The Starbucks logo in Saudi Arabia is just a floating crown. This is because, believe it or not, the original logo featuring a mermaid is far too raunchy to be displayed in the deeply religious and conservative part of the world.

2122. Apple Computers was actually formed by three people, not two. Ronald Wayne was the third co-founder, but in less than a couple weeks, he pulled out of the company, and on April 12th, 1976, Wayne sold his 10% equity in the company for $800. Today, that stake in the company would be worth 62.93 billion dollars.

2123. There are white strawberries with red seeds in Japan called "The Scent of First Love". They are amazingly sweet and rich, but also ridiculously expensive at about $4.10 American per berry!

2124. In 2012, John and Frances Canning invited Queen Elizabeth to their wedding in Manchester as a joke. But astonishingly, the queen surprised them by actually showing up.

2125. Elvis Presley once tipped a limo driver by buying him the same limo that he had been driving him around in.

2126. A businessman named Armand Hammer coincidentally served on a board of directors for Arm & Hammer.

2127. Paul McCartney is the only musician to ever top the charts as a solo artist, and in a duo, trio, quartet, and quintet.

2128. In the music industry, for every $1000 of music sold, the average musician only gets about $23.40.

2129. The IOS game "Clash of Clans" was making an astonishing 1.5 million dollars a day in its peak.

2130. Habitat 67 is a model community and housing complex in Montreal and is considered an architectural landmark as well as being the most recognizable buildings in the city.

2131. Facebook has over one billion users and more than 10,000 of them die every day. Meaning that dead Facebook users will soon outnumber the living ones, which also means that it could become a digital graveyard by the year 2065.

2132. A 20 year old gallon of McDonald's barbecue sauce that was used for the McJordan Burger in the early 1990's sold for almost $10,000 in 2012.

2133. While filming "I am Legend", Will Smith got so attached to his co-star Abbey the German Shepherd, that he asked if he could keep her, but the owner refused.

2134. During World War two, the Soviets built an A-40 Krylya Tanka, a tank with wings. It didn't actually work.

2135. If humans had eagle vision, we'd be able to see an ant crawling on the ground from the roof of a ten story building. In fact, everything would also be brilliantly colored and objects in our line of sight would be magnified.

2136. Phytophotodermatitis, often referred to as "margarita dermatitis", or lyme disease, not to be confused with Lyme disease with a Y, is a toxic reaction resulting from citric acid mixed with sunlight. It can cause second degree burns and is very painful.

2137. The distance from Mars to the Sun is 128 million miles (206 million km) at its closest point. And 154 million miles (250 million km) at it furthest.

2138. According to National Geographic, the Beelzebufo Ampinga, or the "devil frog"may be the largest frog that ever existed. These extinct beach ball sized amphibians grew to almost half a meter long and weighed approximately 10 pounds (4.5 kilograms).

2139. Novice climbers are not allowed to climb Mount Everest according to joint-secretary of Nepal's Ministry of Tourism. In order to qualify to climb it, you are required to have reached the peak of at least one 21,000 feet (6,500 meter) mountain in your lifetime.

2140. Scientists have discovered that there are actually five tastes or senses that your tongue and recognize. They are sweet, sour, salty, bitter, and umami. Parmesan cheese is an example of umami.

2141. From 2010 to 2015, taco bell secretly reduced the sodium content in 33 menu items by 33%, and nobody noticed.

2142. The opposite of deja vu is Jamais vu. It's a French word meaning "never seen." It's a feeling or experience when a person knows or recognizes a situation, but still feels very unfamiliar and unknown to them.

2143. In 1965, Mattel released Slumber Party Barbie. Apparently, one of her slumber party essentials was a pink scale that was permanently set to 110 pounds (50 kg).

2144. Makoto Igarashi from Tokyo developed a Hizamakura Lap Pillow, which is a cushion shaped like a woman's legs wearing a mini-skirt, that you can lay your head down on for maternal feelings.

2145. During World War II, Germany used guns that had a curved barrel device that was clamped onto the end of an MP44 rifle that allowed soldiers to shoot over obstacles without exposing themselves to return fire.

2146. Sea scallops have about 60 eyes. They can be a bright blue color and help the scallop detect light, dark, and motion.

2147. Boxer Muhammad Ali's star on the Walk of Fame is on the wall, not on the pavement because he didn't want the name of Muhammad to be stepped on.

2148. Writer and director Oliver Stone received a Purple Heart and Bronze Star for his service in the Vietnam War.

2149. Breastfed babies poop more than formula fed babies because breast milk contains immunoglobulins, substances produced by the body's immune system which works like a natural laxative.

2150. According to the Centers for Disease Control and Prevention, or the CDC, as of 2014, one in 68 children, or more specifically, one in 42 boys and one in 189 girls, has autism spectrum disorder, which includes a wide range of symptoms, skills in different levels of disability.

2151. In 2014, scientists discover the earliest evidence of human footprints. These were outside of Africa on the Norfolk coast in the east of England. The footprints were found on the shores of Happisburgh and were more than 800,000 years old.

2152. Every single spring, Sweetwater, Texas, has a rattlesnake round-up. For three days, snake hunters bring in their catches, which end up being 1000's of snakes, for which they're paid five dollars for every pound. The junior Chamber of Commerce began the tradition back in 1958 to address the overpopulation of snakes.

2153. In Indonesia, whole smoked bats are considered a delicacy.

2154. When important Vikings died, they were put into a burial ship along with their clothes and jewelry, where they were either buried or set on fire and pushed out to sea.

2155. The fear of clowns is called "coulrophobia", and has increased significantly over the last 20 years due to their portrayal in popular culture and the recent scary clown phenomenon where people have been dressing up as clowns to scare others.

2156. If your parents or grandparents have a history of multiple cavities or dentures at an early age, you have a higher risk of the same thing due to genetics.

2157. Frogs can't swallow with their eyes open.

2158. On March 26th, 1976, Queen Elizabeth sent her first email. The message was transmitted over ARPANET, the forerunner for the modern internet. She is considered the first head of state to have used electronic mail.

2159. Tony Iommi started down-tuning his guitar after an accident that cut the end of his two fingers off, thus creating Black Sabbath's signature sound.

2160. Elle King, singer of 'Ex's and Oh's' is actor Rob Schneider's daughter.

2161. Michael Jordan's number 23 was retired by the Miami Heat, even though he has never played for them.

2162. Dogs feel most vulnerable when they're pooping, so they look to their owners for protection, which often results in awkward staring.

2163. The name LEGO was an abbreviation for the two Danish words "leg godt", meaning "play well."

2164. In 1989, Disney forced three daycare centers to remove a mural of Mickey, Donald, and Goofy, under threat of legal action.

2165. The reality show 'The Voice' has yet to create any new singing stars, but has effectively rejuvenated the careers of its celebrity judges.

2166. It's estimated that the Mexican Drug Cartel Caballeros Templarios, or 'The Knights Templar', makes $152 million a year from growing and selling avocados.

2167. Mexican jumping beans get their jump from moth larvae inside the pod that twitches when abruptly warmed.

2168. In 1723, French Naval Officer Gabriel de Clieu carried a single coffee seedling all the way from France to Martinique, a Caribbean island, where it spread and birthed 18 million trees over 50 years. Eventually, those trees made it to South and Central America.

2169. Elephants have the longest known pregnancy of any animal, lasting up to 680 days. In addition to being born with an advanced level of brain development, they also have a unique cycle of ovulation and hormone levels that are unlike any other animal.

2170. Dr. Wuzong Zhou of St. Andrews University found that about 1.5 million diamond nanoparticles are created in a candle flame every second that it burns. Unfortunately, they're burned away during the process; however, it's believed that this discovery could lead to research into how diamonds could be created more cheaply.

2171. Because the main purpose of marriage to ancient people was to produce children, they used to shower the new bride with fertility symbols like wheat grain. The Romans used to bake this wheat into small cakes to be eaten in a tradition known as "confarreatio", meaning "eating together". The guests of the ceremony used to throw handfuls of honey-eyed nuts and dried fruits called confetto; and this was how the tradition of throwing confetti at weddings started.

2172. The origin of the game hopscotch began in ancient Britain during the Roman Empire. The original courts were 30 meters long and were used for military training exercises. Soldiers actually used to run in full armor and field packs to improve their footwork. Roman children drew their own, smaller courts and added a scoring system; and thus, hopscotch was born and spread throughout Europe.

2173. The 2011 Japan earthquake was so powerful that it actually changed the Earth's rotation on its axis, and shortened the day by 1.8 milliseconds.

2174. The largest hidden Mickey Mouse is in Mickey's forest. A 60-acre forest near Walt Disney World, containing over 50,000 pine trees.

2175. The letter Q is the only letter in the alphabet that doesn't appear in any U.S. territory or state name.

2176. Australia has the largest resource of uranium in the world at 31%. At around 12% of the world's annual production, they are the world's third-largest producer behind Kazakhstan and Canada.

2177. Up until 2013, if you were found to be trafficking drugs in Singapore, you were given a mandatory death sentence. As far as harsh drug laws are concerned, Singapore had and still has some of the toughest out of any country in the world.

2178. There's a hotel in Bolivia called the "Palacio de Sal Resort" that is made up of one million 14-inch blocks of compressed grains of salt. Even the furniture is made out of salt.

2179. Mahatma Gandhi never won the Nobel Peace Prize, despite being nominated five times between 1937 and 1948, this despite being one of the strongest symbols for nonviolence in the world and being one of the most respected.

2180. Horses can actually sleep while standing up. This is because of the way that their legs are built. They have ligaments and a structure that allows them to doze off without collapsing.

2181. Believe it or not, fishing was the activity that accounted for the most lightning strikes and deaths between 2006 and 2012. In fact, there were a total of 26 fishing deaths because of it.

2182. Vultures with GoPros and GPS trackers are used to find illegal trash dumps in Peru.

2183. 27 animals died on set throughout the filming of 'The Hobbit' trilogy. Some animals fell into sink holes, while other smaller ones such as chickens, and were killed by unsupervised dogs. The events led to PETA to have a global protest of the trilogy.

2184. In the late 1990s, the Coca Cola Company began testing vending machines that could automatically raise prices for its drinks in hot weather.

2185. Recycling one aluminum can saves enough energy to run a television for three hours.

2186. There is a 30-foot replica of a 1951 Canadian nickel in Sudbury, Ontario, Canada.

2187. At birth, baby kangaroos or joeys can be as small as a grain of rice or as big as a bee.

2188. 3.5 billion years ago, a mega-asteroid that was likely 30 miles across slammed into Earth in Australia.

2189. As of May 10th, 2016, the Endangered Species Act of 1973 listed 1,367 species of animals and 901 species of plants as endangered or threatened.

2190. The horned lizard has blood-filled sinuses within the eye sockets that squirt blood in self-defense by swelling and rupturing.

2191. In 2012, the street artist, Megx converted an old bridge in Wuppertal, Germany into a giant Lego structure using colored panels to create the illusion of the underside of Lego bricks.

2192. In most European countries, including Britain, declawing your cat is illegal. If you're caught declawing a cat in Israel, you can actually be sent to jail for a year and be fined 20 thousand dollars. Scotland, Italy, New Zealand, and over 30 other countries have also followed suit.

2193. In New Zealand, it's illegal to own just one guinea pig because they are very lonely and social creatures. In fact, they have matchmaking companies to match up your guinea pig if their partner dies, which is part of a sweeping animals' rights legislation that was first introduced in 2008.

2194. If you live in Australia, you are 20 times more likely to drown than be bitten by a shark. In fact, to put it into perspective, you're significantly more likely to win the top prize in the lottery than even being involved in a shark accident of any kind.

2195. According to the World Health Organization, there are 360 million people in the world with disabling hearing loss. That's around five percent of the entire world's population with 32 million of them being children between the ages of zero and 14.

2196. On July 13th, 1955, nightclub owner, Ruth Ellis was the last woman to be executed for murder in Great Britain. She was hanged for killing her boyfriend, and it wasn't until 1965 that the death penalty for murder was banned in England, Scotland, and Wales.

2197. A study in the Journal of Current Biology found that those people who exercise four hours after learning something new, retained the information better two days later than those who exercise immediately or not at all.

2198. Ringling Bros Barnum and Bailey Circus have retired all elephants in their show as of May 1st, 2016. All of the elephants will go to Florida conservation, where they can help with cancer research, as they possess a special P53 gene, which helps fight cancer.

2199. There is something called "geographic tongue", which is actually a real health condition, with a map-like feature across your tongue, and in some cases, entire mouth.

2200. The mineral Jadarite, discovered in a Serbian mine, has the same chemical composition as Kryptonite that has been described in the Superman movies.

2201. Every week, about 50 cats and dogs are transported from Houston to Colorado in order to avoid euthanization.

2202. Male platypuses have venomous spurs, and can even sense electromagnetic fields just like a fish.

2203. Sir Isaac Newton predicted that the world would end in 2060.

2204. The animated film 'Sleeping Beauty' took so long to make, that Walt Disney grew bored of it, and actually redirected his energy into the creation of Disneyland. In fact, the iconic Sleeping Beauty's castle was built at the center of the park as promotion for that film's eventual debut just four years later.

2205. As a 12 year old, Shia LaBeouf found an agent in the Yellow Pages, and was taken on after pretending to be his own manager.

2206. Originally, the traffic and train light for go was white, and caution was green. The choice of white light for go turned out to cause a lot of problems. For example, back in 1914, one of the red lenses fell out of its holder while leaving a white light behind it exposed. This ended up with a train running a stop signal and crashing into another train; so the railroad changed it so that the green light means go, and yellow was chosen for caution mostly because it's the most distinct color from the other two.

2207. Over the past decade, our complete obsession with bacon has led to some seriously strange bacon products. Some examples of this include bacon ice cream, bacon lollipops, bacon mayonnaise, bacon chocolate bars and, yes, bacon gumballs.

2208. Netflix has actually made a Netflix and chill button called "The Switch," when you activate it, The Switch dims the lights, activates your phone's do-not-disturb feature, and gets Netflix ready for streaming.

2209. Spiders cannot digest solid food. Before they can eat their prey, they must turn their meal into a liquid form. They exude digestive enzymes from their stomach onto the victim's body. Once the enzymes break down the tissues of the prey, they suck up the liquid remains.

2210. The national animal of Scotland is the unicorn.

2211. There is an island in the Bahamas known as Pig Beach, which is populated entirely by pigs. Visitors can actually arrange to swim with them.

2212. It is against the law to disrupt a wedding or funeral in South Australia.

2213. A Swedish tourism agency created The Swedish Number, 46 771 793 336, a single phone line that connects international callers to randomly-selected Swedish volunteers to chat about whatever's on their minds.

2214. iPhone owners unlock their device, on average, about 80 times per day.

2215. Slash didn't actually purchase his iconic top hat. He shoplifted it from a store. He just put it on his head and walked out.

2216. Qatar Airways allows you to travel with and keep a falcon in the cabin, provided that there aren't already six falcons aboard.

2217. The orange stitching on the back pockets of Levi jeans is called "arcuate". Since the design has literally no function, it was painted on during World War II rationing.

2218. President John Quincy Adams had a pet alligator. He kept it in the bathtub in the East Room of the White House.

2219. Back in the mid-2000s, Kim Kardashian used to be Paris Hilton's personal assistant.

2220. About 25% to 40% of people have motion sickness. According to the University of Maryland Medical Center, women are more susceptible than men and Asians are more susceptible than white or black people.

2221. According to the Guinness World Records, the longest videogame marathon playing World of Warcraft was 29 hours and 31 minutes. This was achieved by Hecaterina Kinumi Iglesias, a.k.a. Kinumi Cati, in Vigo, Spain, on the 29th to 30th of March, back in 2014.

2222. There is an over-50-kilometer-long tunnel that connects the United Kingdom to Europe. It's called the "Channel Tunnel", or "Chunnel", and is located underneath the English Channel. The trip underneath through the channel takes only about 30 minutes and in fact, an entire trip to London to Paris is only two hours and 15 minutes.

If you enjoyed this book at all it would mean the world to me if you could please leave a quick review so others can quench their trivia curiosity! Thank you so much in advance!!

CPSIA information can be obtained
at www.ICGtesting.com
Printed in the USA
FSHW011254200520
70430FS